LIFE STORY OF
SANT ATTAR SINGH JI

By the same author :

LIFE STORY OF
SANT ATTAR SINGH JI
[OF MASTUANA SAHIB]

HARBANS SINGH DOABIA

Singh Brothers
Amritsar

LIFE STORY OF SANT ATTAR SINGH JI
by
HARBANS SINGH DOABIA

ISBN 81-7205-072-0

First Edition July 1992
Second Edition September 1999
Third Edition October 2006

Price : Rs. 80-00

Publishers :
Singh Brothers
●
Bazar Mai Sewan, Amritsar - 143 006
●
S.C.O. 223-24, City Centre, Amritsar - 143 001
E-mail : singhbro@vsnl.com
Website : www.singhbrothers.com

Printers :
PRINTWELL, 146, INDUSTRIAL FOCAL POINT, AMRITSAR.

CONTENTS

PREFACE

Many True Sikh Saints have been appearing in this world to spread the most Sacred Mission of Sri Satguru Nanak Dev from time to time. Unfortunately we have not done much to tell others about the life stories of our Satgurus and True Saints, which give real guidance to all. To preach True Sikh Religion and History is most essential to save all from the so-called modern thought and civilisation which is dragging the world towards the burning deep sea of sins and evil ways.

The Divine Order of God and the Satgurus is that we must examine the Limitless Stories of the Spiritual and Divine Treasury, which we have inherited from our Great Gurus. Our Satgurus give the title of 'True Sons' to those worthy devotees, who tell others the life stories of their ancestors. Kindly see as to what efforts are being made by us in this direction.

Sant Attar Singh Ji of Mastuana is one of the True Saints, who preached the Sikh Religion from place to place throughout India and caused it to be preached in foreign countries also. Particularly through Sant Teja Singh Ji M.A. whom he sent abroad. He administered the Nectar of the double-edged sword to lakhs of misguided devotees of the Sikh Gurus. He also spread the message of the fatherhood of God and the brotherhood of man.

In fact, the establishment of so many Sikh Educational Institutions is mainly the result of his unending efforts to spread true education everywhere. The Sikh

Educational Conferences were also held almost every year, due to his miraculous influence. His influence even on non-Sikhs is wonderful.

In this small book, very humble efforts are made to give brief life story of this great Saint. Some Sermons based on Gurbani, which he delivered have not been printed. Many subjects, such as to what is the need of True Saints as to who is a True Saint, as to what is Salvation, as to who is True and Pure Khalsa (and many more topics) have also not been printed in this Edition of the book. With the Grace of the Satguru, these will be printed subsequently.

We do not want to write a long preface; but we most humbly want to assert the following points for the due consideration and proper action of all the well-wishers of the Panth and all others :

a) Are all our Educational Institutions carrying out the programs according to the directions of our Satgurus ?

b) What is the difference between the non-Sikh so-called modern public schools and educational institutions and the Sikh Educational Institutions ?

c) Why is the younger generation, generally speaking not paying due respect to the elders ?

d) What steps are being taken by us to stop further pollution of the mind, which are already covered with thick layers of pitch dark cover of the sins etc., since the previous births ?

e) How far are we obeying the most mandatory Command of the Satguru that we must not follow those ways and programs, which cause us to forget our Satgurus and God ?

We beg to point out that the modern writers are

giving distorted facts about our Great Religion and our History. The book, containing some of the True Stories (Sakhis), Dialogues and Sermons after consulting many respected writers such as Bhai Sahib Bhai Gurdas Ji, Bhai Sahib Bhai Santokh Singh Ji, Bhai Sahib Bhai Vir Singh Ji, Bhai Sahib Bhai Mani Singh Ji and Puratan Janam Sakhis, etc. will be published soon.

It is rather sad that disrespectful remarks are made in some of the books written regarding our Satgurus and Religion by some persons. We have made very little efforts to undo the wrongs done by these writers.

Kindly excuse us for our shortcomings. We will be glad to get kind suggestions of the learned readers.

31.3.1992   HUMBLE AUTHOR
2771, Phase VII, Mohali,
Distt. Ropar, Punjab, India.
Tele. 570887

Chapter I

THE BIRTH AND CHILDHOOD

Sant Attar Singh Ji was born in village Cheema (then in Patiala State, but now in the Sangrur District of Punjab); on the Chet Sudi Ekam, 1923 Bikrami (28th March, 1867 A.D.). The name of his mother was (Mata) Bholi and that of his father was (Baba) Karam Singh, who used to earn his livelihood by tilling land.

When Sant Ji was able to walk a little, he would many times sit in some corner of the room of the house. The mother used to become worried, as to where the child had gone. When he was two and a half years old, he used to utter very sweet words. His talk was enchanting. He developed a great respect for his elder sister (Bibi) Rattan Kaur. He had a strong yearning to continue sitting in meditation for long periods.

When Sant Ji was seven years of age, the father wanted to send him to a school. Sant Ji humbly told his father that he would read the "Language and subjects of God" (The True Being) and would not read Persian or English. At this, the father sent him to the Dera (hermitage) of Bhai Ram Singh Ji, Nirmala. There, the teacher, named Bhai Buta Singh, began teaching him Gurmukhi and Divine Hymns (Gurbani).

After sometime, the father directed Sant Ji to graze the cattle. He would take them to the fields, but would never strike them with a stick. He used to touch them mildly, with his towel, in order to goad them. He would take his mates to the fields. They would sit under some tree and would start meditating. When the cattle used to stray to other's fields, they would be brought back immediately by his mates. Sant Ji used to pay respects to saintly figures.

As desired by (Baba) Karam Singh Ji, when Sant Ji passed the stage of childhood, he began cultivating land. While doing so, he would, many times, sit aloof and would begin meditation on God and His Name. The parents were not happy at this and would discuss as to how their son would earn livelihood in future. One day, the father requested the son, "You please do the work of agriculture with full vigour." He smiled and said that he would engage himself soon in some more beneficial pursuits.

CHAPTER II

JOINED ARMY—LEFT FOR HAZUR SAHIB WITHOUT LEAVE

Sant Ji soon joined the army and was posted at Kohat in the Artillery Regiment, where he remained for one year.

He remained a bachelor and refused to be married. He has a very great yearning to go to Hazur Sahib. So he left the regiment and started on foot for Hazur Sahib. From his childhood he had no attachment with worldly affairs and he remained thinking of Gurbani, Naam,

Gurus and Akal Purakh even in childhood.

He started on foot from Kohat, throughout meditating on the Naam. His mind became ever fixed upon the Shabad. He continued travelling on foot, day and night, in this way. Sometimes, he would take some rest and would prepare his food after taking flour etc., from some Gurdwaras in the way. His mind continued to yearn to reach the sacred Gurdwara of Hazur Sahib and to rub the sacred dust of that place on his body. He would utter 'Wah' while lifting his left foot and 'Guru' while lifting his right foot.

In due course, Sant Ji reached Abchal Nagar (Hazur Sahib) Gurdwara. He at once entered the Gurdwara, after necessary ablutions and bowed before the Satguru in a most respectful way and obeyed the mandate. He had already surrendered his body, mind and riches and all that he possessed before the True Guru.

Stayed at Nagina Ghat for one year and seven months

He now began to stay at the Nagina Ghat near the River Godavari. After a few days, he began to tie a small turban of coarse cloth (Khaddar) on his head and put off all other clothes, except the Kachhera (the prescribed underwear). He would keep a small towel with him.

Continuous Meditation began

He now began constant meditation i.e., worship of God and His Name. If some food was given, he would take it, otherwise he remained contented by sipping the water of river Godavari. He had given strict order that only one leaf of bread with some cooked pulses, placed on it, should be brought for him. This was complied with by his attendant. In this way, he stayed at Nagina Ghat for about one year and seven months. During his stay at Nagina Ghat, he would spend nights in a small stone-built hut, where he would remain engaged in meditation. He would repeat the Fundamental Spell accompanied by some more Hymns. These countless recitations etc., were unique in themselves. He would not talk with anyone during this period. He was most humble and would fall at the feet of any Sikh, who came to meet him. Even if somebody uttered harsh words, he would remain silent. He would sweep the main Gurdwara Sahib (Darbar Sahib) with a broom and would bring water for its necessary holy wash.

Some of the True Stories

One day, Sant Ji Maharaj started walking on the bank of the River Godavari. At a distance of nearly three miles, he began self-mortification, in meditation for nearly ten days without food. Bhai Nanu Singh, the head Poojari of Darbar Sahib, saw a vision one night, and heard the Divine Voice saying, "Our dear Sikh is standing in meditation in the river for the last eight days without any food. Serve him food."

Next morning, Bhai Nanu Singh cooked food and walked on the bank of the river for about two miles, but finding none returned back. On the same night, he again heard in the vision, "You have not served food to our beloved Sikh." He replied, "Sir, I tried to contact him, but could not find him anywhere." Then the voice said, "Walk for about three miles and then you would find him." On the following morning, he again took food and went for nearly three miles on the bank of the river. Now he saw Sant Ji Maharaj, standing in the knee-deep water. When Sant Ji Maharaj opened his eyes, he saw Bhai Nanu Singh and enquired, "How have you come here ?" He told all the details of his dream and offered food to Sant Ji Maharaj. He refused to eat anything. Bhai Nanu Singh then said, "I shall not be able to sleep. Kindly accept my humble offer." Then Sant Ji warned Bhai Nanu Singh not to tell anybody about this episode and he took some food.

Cobra came to pay respects

Once, when Sant Ji Maharaj was in deep meditation at Gautam Ghat, the attendant, who brought food for him, noticed a very big cobra sitting near Sant Ji Maharaj with its hood fully spread. The attendant became horrified first, but when he reached near Sant Ji, the cobra left the place. Sant Ji Maharaj opened his eyes and observed, "This beloved being came to give its glimpse to me."

He jumped in the river but he was saved

Sant Ji in due course, visited and paid homage at all the Gurdwaras near Hazur Sahib. He visited these on foot. Now nearly two years had passed in meditation at Hazur Sahib. He was extremely anxious to see the sight of the tenth Satguru, but did not succeed in this. One day, he decided to jump in the deep water of river Godavari so that his physical body should be sacrificed before the Satguru. He immediately jumped in it; but some mysterious power took him alive on the bank and observed, "You are my Sikh. Be alert. You have to give Khande-da-Amrit to many persons in the Punjab and other places. You have to spread the message of peace in the entire world with the help of Sat-Naam (The True Word)." He also Heard, "If you want to have my sight, come at Nagina Ghat at midnight." Sant Ji anxiously waited for this moment. When he reached Nagina Ghat at midnight, he saw the Tenth Satguru sitting on a throne surrounded by the five Beloved, the four sons and many others. Sant Ji prostrated and paid all respects. As to what happened subsequently is not told to anyone by Sant Ji.

A few days after this, Sant Ji Maharaj decided to return to Punjab. He offered respectful prayers for safe return etc. Bhai Nanu Singh offered, as a respectful gift, some clothes to Sant Ji Maharaj, but he refused to take these.

CHAPTER III

VISITED HARDWAR AND OTHER PLACES

He then started his journey on foot for Hardwar and Rikhikesh. Although he did not want to leave Hazur Sahib, where he had obtained the Grace of Satguru Gobind Singh Ji Maharaj, yet in view of his command to serve the world, he started his long journey on foot, after performing Ardas (prayers at Darbar Sahib) to visit Hardwar.

Big Tiger came and paid respects

He passed through very thick jungle of the central India. Bhai Bhagat Singh accompanied him. One day, they saw a very big tiger while crossing the jungles. Bhai Bhagat Singh was terrified, but Sant Ji Maharaj remained perfectly calm and continued his journey. When the tiger came near Sant Ji, it saw his brilliant face. Sant Ji threw his affectionate nectarean glimpses on it. Now the tiger felt joy at this and went away like a cat in the jungle. Sant Ji Maharaj observed, "Bhai Bhagat Singh, the knower of all hearts had come to give us His sight."

He reached Khandwa and Ajmer

After travelling through the central India, Sant Ji Maharaj reached Khandwa and then Ajmer. Sant Ji Maharaj then reached Hardwar. He stayed there for some days and then went to Rikhikesh.

Continuous Meditation at Hardwar and Rikhikesh

At Hardwar, as well as at Rikhikesh, Sant Ji used to get up before 2.00 a.m. He would remain in deep meditation till noon. He would then eat very little food. He did not talk with anyone. If a loaf of bread was not procured, he would sip a little water. He would again begin meditation after this and would continue worship of God till late in the night. He would take little or no rest.

Visited spring where tigers used to come

One day, he went up to the spring where during night, tigers used to come to drink water. Here he sat in deep meditation. Many tigers came and went away, after drinking water, but none even touched him. Early morning, he came back.

Sant Ji stayed at Rikhikesh for more than a year. Sant Ji left Rikhikesh and came to Paonta Sahib. He then visited Nahan. At these places he paid respects at all the Gurdwaras of Satguru Gobind Singh Ji Maharaj. He then went to Sialkot. He visited Gurdwara Ber Sahib and stayed at the Dera of Sant Ram Singh.

He visited Amritsar—Meditation at Baba Attal

In due course, he came to Sri Amritsar Sahib and paid respects at Darbar Sahib. Then he went on the third floor of Gurdwara Baba Attal Sahib. For three days, he remained in deep meditation here. On the fourth day a Sikh brought food and rice cooked in milk. Now, Sant Ji Maharaj remained silent in strange joy for sometime. Then that Sikh requested him to take food, which he took with pleasure.

CHAPTER IV

DISCHARGE FROM ARMY—THEN VISITED MANY PLACES—PERFORMED VERY LONG MEDITATIONS

Sant Ji now decided that he must get himself discharged from his regiment. So he came to Abbot Abad and told the Colonel that he should be relieved.

Sant Ji was sent to Quarter Guard, where he continued to be absorbed in meditation. Now the Colonel reluctantly passed the discharged order and gave Sant Ji the amount of prize that he had already won and bade him farewell.

When Sant Ji came out, he distributed the said amount amongst poorer persons and made preparations for leaving Abbot Abad. All the soldiers bade farewell and showed all respects. Sant Ji Maharaj took a tonga. The tonga started and Sant Ji Maharaj became engaged in paying respects to the Satguru, offering thanks to him.

Sant Ji reached Havelian in the evening.

Here Bhai Gurmukh Singh paid respects to Sant Ji, when he was passing through the Bazar. On his request Sant Ji agreed to stay at his house. He occupied a part of the room in which Sri Guru Granth Sahib was kept by Bhai Gurmukh Singh. Sant Ji began reciting Divine Hymns from the beginning to the end of Sri Guru Granth Sahib and then performed Bhog (closing ceremony). After one Path, he commenced another one and continued to perform continuous reading of Sri Guru Granth Sahib one after the other for nine months. Then he left for Panja Sahib.

Sant Ji paid great respects at the Gurdwara Panja Sahib. After this, he went to Dumel and sat in meditation at the place where river Jehlum and river Kishan Ganga meet together. Then he went to Koh Murry, at which place he tried to search for a very high peak, where he would sit in meditation. He found a very high peak, where there was complete solitude. There was no population for miles around this peak. He sat in meditation for three days. On the fourth day, he saw an old lady sitting near him. She had two thick loaves made of cornflour, on which some cooked vegetable was placed. He then ate the two loaves and thanked the Satguru.

Sant Ji then decided to go to Kanoha. He liked the grove of trees at that place, where there was lot of water also. Opposite the Gurdwara of village Kanoha was the house of Bhai Wazir Singh. He and his wife Bhag Bhari used to serve the Sadhus. They now began serving Sant Attar Singh Ji with full devotion. One day, their son fell ill. Bhag Bhari desired that an Akhand Path (continuous reading) of Sri Guru Granth Sahib might be performed by Sant Ji. Wazir Singh saw Sant Ji and submitted, "Sir, we want to get performed Akhand Path of Sri Guru Granth Sahib. Kindly grace the occasion."

Akhand Path (continuous recitation of Sri Guru Granth Sahib) for three days performed by Sant Ji Maharaj alone

Sant Ji did not give any reply; but followed him and reached the Gurdwara. He sat on the dais, where Sri Guru Granth Sahib was placed, after necessary ablutions. Now the person, who had to recite Jap Ji Sahib, also came. The Sangat (Sikhs) gathered in the Gurdwara. The reading of the Akhand Path began at 10 a.m. In the most magical, enchanting and loud voice, Sant Ji Maharaj read the whole of the Granth Sahib, all alone. The reading could be heard up to a distance of half a mile. Sant Ji stayed at the Gurdwara for 2/3 days. Many Sikhs began visiting the Gurdwara to pay respects to him. He now decided to leave the Gurdwara.

He sat in meditation for five days without food

One night, at about 1 a.m., Sant Ji went inside the thick grove of wild trees, without telling anybody. A very big snake used to live here. He sat in meditation. Now sun came over the head of Sant Ji. Bhai Wazir Singh thought of erecting a thatched cottage for Sant Ji Maharaj. Sant Ji permitted Bhai Wazir Singh to erect the cottage. After the cottage was built, he took his seat in it.

Big serpent paid respects to Sant Ji Maharaj

One day, Buta Singh, the younger brother of Bhai Wazir Singh went to the side of the grove. He saw a very big serpent there. He was so much terrified on seeing it, that he ran to the Gurdwara and loudly proclaimed that the serpent had eaten the 'Sadhu'. Sant Ji was quite safe and sound and he told the Sangat that the serpent came to pay respects to him.

Bhai Wazir Singh used to daily bring food for Sant Ji Maharaj, Who told him, "Please see that the loaves of bread prepared for me should be with the flour prepared from your own corns and not from the corns that you receive from others, as payments of your debts etc. Honestly earned bread does not cause disturbance in the mind, while sitting in meditation."

One day Sant Ji asked Wazir Singh to build a small room near the water reservoir in the grove and to place a cot inside it, for Sri Guru Granth Sahib there. This was complied with. Now Sri Guru Granth Sahib was brought there. Bhai Wazir Singh and his wife requested Sant Ji to allow to give a big feast (Langar) to all. This request was allowed. Now all the necessary things such as flour etc., were brought by Bhai Wazir Singh. Everything was prepared. Langar (Free Kitchen) was ready. The Sangat (Sikhs) had gathered in large numbers. Wazir Singh thought that Karah Parshad (Sacred Pudding) etc., would not be sufficient to serve all. Sant Ji told him not to worry on this account. As ordered by him, a sheet of cloth was spread over the food and over the Karah Parshad. Now the distribution of the food etc. began. Sant Ji himself sat near the place where Langar was stored. This was distributed to all till the evening and the Sangat took away some of it even to their homes. Even cows and buffaloes were given food, to their fill. This was a miracle that the Langar was distributed in abundance. Wazir Singh and his wife Bhag Bhari came to thank and pay respects to Sant Ji Maharaj, who observed that this was due to the kindness of the Satguru.

Long meditation at Kanoha

After this function, Sant Ji Maharaj went to his hut. He began decreasing his daily food for six days and on the evening of the seventh day he totally stopped taking food. He bolted from inside the door of the hut. Wazir Singh and his wife used to daily come to serve food but they found the door closed and had to return back after waiting for the whole of the day. In this way forty days passed away. On the forty-first day, Sant Ji Maharaj opened the door of the hut and observed from inside that he had done so to relieve the anxiety of the couple. For two months, he remained outside, but he had told them that he would continuously sit in meditation for six months in the cottage.

Six months' meditation

After two months, he again began reducing his food and on the eighth day he did not take anything. When the couple insisted that Sant Ji Maharaj might agree to take some little food etc., each day during the period of his long meditation for six months, he agreed to this, "You may bring a quarter seer of milk in the morning and a little cold drink prepared by grinding almonds etc. in the evening and place these outside the cottage. Also leave one green twig for my use as a tooth brush each evening. Never try to come inside."

The very next day, Sant Ji bolted the door of the cottage from inside. After six months, when Bhai Wazir Singh and his wife Bhag Bhari came to the cottage, they found its door open. They came inside and found that Sant Ji was much reduced. They shampooed his body with clarified butter. Then they slowly brought Sant Ji Maharaj outside and put butter on his head and rubbed it. They found that at that time his long hair had become so long that these touched his feet. Sant Ji Maharaj observed, "I had got so much spiritual pleasure at this place that I would like to sit in meditation at this place for one year continuously."

On the insistence and requests of the couple, Sant Ji agreed to remain outside for four months.

One year's meditation

Four months passed off easily. Sant Ji then began reducing his food day by day for twelve days. He told the couple that he would sit in meditation for full one year. The couple prayed that permission might be granted to leave some food outside. Sant Ji at last agreed to this and observed, "Bring a little milk early morning. In the afternoon bring cold drink prepared by grinding almonds etc. In the evening bring a small bowl of cooked vegetables. Nothing more is needed. These should be placed in the outer niche of the cottage." On the request of the couple, Sant Ji agreed that some curd for washing the long hair should be left after every week. Next day was Baisakhi day. Sant Ji Maharaj bolted the door of the cottage from inside and began continuous meditation for one year, at about 2 a.m. After full one year, early before sunrise, on the Baisakhi day of Sambat 1953, Sant Ji Maharaj opened the door of the cottage. Large number of Sikhs had already gathered there. They were highly pleased to see Sant Ji hale and hearty, when they went inside the cottage. Although his body had become very weak, yet there was a Divine Glow on his face. The Sangat fell at his feet. They slowly and delicately shampooed the body of Sant Ji. They brought him outside the cottage. He smiled and observed, "I had not been working at the plough. I am not tired. Do not worry on my account." Bhai Wazir Singh submitted, "Sir, you have been working at the *'biggest plough'* in as much as, you have done all this for the peace and benefit of the world and whole mankind.

CHAPTER V

SOME TRUE STORIES OF THAT PERIOD

Story of Prem Singh

After this, Sant Ji wanted to keep some true companions with him. One day, while going towards the grove, from the house of Bhai Wazir Singh, Sant Ji saw a washerman named Prem Singh, washing others' clothes. He was also reciting orally the Divine Hymn (Sukhmani Sahib). Sant Ji asked him, "You are a devoted Sikh. Why are you washing the dirt of others ?" On hearing this, Bhai Prem Singh followed Sant Ji Maharaj and fell at his feet. He submitted, "Sir, my hands are twisted. I earn my livelihood by doing this work. No one will give food to me, if I remain idle." On this, Sant Ji observed, "On your forehead, it is written that you will engage yourself in devotional meditation and then food etc. will automatically follow you."

Now Prem Singh began worshipping God and Satguru day and night. With the Grace of Sant Ji, Prem Singh became a Giani (Knower of Divine Matters).

Sant Ji left Kanoha. When after some years Sant Ji Maharaj came here, Bhai Prem Singh was with him. Sant

Ji began giving a discourse after reciting a Divine Hymn in the morning, explaining its meanings. At that time Bhai Prem Singh was sitting in the back-room of the Gurdwara. He loudly spoke, "Sant Ji, you have committed a mistake." Sant Ji Maharaj observed, "Gurbani (Divine Hymns) of Sri Guru Granth Sahib is beyond the comprehension of a mortal. Its correct meaning cannot be written or explained by anybody. You have now become Giani. You please remain aloof from me." From that day, Prem Singh left Sant Ji for sometime. Then he came to perform physical service of the Gurdwara Gursagar Mastuana, but he had to go to Kanjla from this place after sometime. Bhai Baj Singh, Bhai Kalyan Singh and Bhai Buta Singh became Sevaks (followers) of Sant Ji Maharaj at Kanoha and performed meditation and worship with devotion.

Prophecy of Baba Khem Singh

One day, Baba Khem Singh came to Kanoha on his usual tour. According to his habit, he came to shoot some birds etc., in the thick grove of Kanoha. Sant Ji Maharaj was lying asleep there and his feet were not covered at that time. Baba Khem Singh was very fond of meeting saints and Sadhus. He did not think it advisable to wake up Sant Ji Maharaj. When he came to the village and talked about this with his followers and devotees, he learnt that Sant Ji had performed continuous meditations three times. They narrated the whole story. Baba Khem Singh observed, "This Sant will be the True King of the whole world."

Baba Khem Singh was now anxious to meet Sant Ji. Bhai Wazir Singh had invited Baba Ji to take his meals in his house on that day. He ordered Wazir Singh not to kill a goat for serving meat and that vegetarian food should be prepared. He wanted Sant Ji to come on the occasion and sit with him for taking food. At the appointed time, Baba Ji came with his followers and Sant Ji also came there. Baba Ji requested Sant Ji to sit near him. When the food was being served, Sant Ji observed, "Why have you prohibited the cooking of usual food for you ?" Baba Ji replied politely, "This did not look nice, when I have to take meals with you." Baba Ji got stopped killing of goats as long as he remained at Kanoha and Sant Ji was invited to come from the grove everyday and take food with him.

Bitter water became sweet

There was a *kacha* well in front of the house of Bhai Wazir Singh. Sant Ji observed, "Get it built with bricks and mortar." His wife replied, "Sir, the water of the well is bitter." One day, Sant Ji Maharaj took in his hands some water of the well and threw it and observed, "Get it built *pacca*. The water is sweet." This was complied with. Its water became very sweet.

Old Lady liberated

After the third period of meditation, Sant Ji started taking food in the house of Wazir Singh. Many other devotees wanted to invite him to take food in their house. One day, Sant Ji was going to the house of Pandit Sham Singh for taking food. Two more persons were with him. In the way fell the house of Bhai Kalyan Singh Kohli. His mother Dheron was lying on the bed outside. She got up and caught the feet of Sant Ji who wanted her to leave him. The old woman said, "Sir, I am very ill. I am in great pain. My son has turned me out of the house in this miserable condition. Death does not come." Sant Ji

Maharaj heard this painful story and expressed great pity for her. He observed, "You will leave this world tomorrow at this time."

Refusal to take food in all houses

When Sant Ji Maharaj went to the house of Wazir Singh, he refused to take food which was placed before him and observed in the evening, when Sangat had gathered, "I have felt much, when I saw the old woman. In future, I will not go to take food in any other house. I cannot repay the debts of so many persons. It is enough for me, if I can do so in the case of one person only." He ordered Bhag Bhari to cook food for him everyday and he used to take it in her house only. On the next day, Sant Ji Maharaj sent a man to find the condition of the old woman. He came and told Sant Ji Maharaj that she had expired. After this, Sant Ji Maharaj did not go to any other house to take food.

Snake appeared to hear Gurbani

One day, Sant Ji was singing Divine Hymns and the entire Sangat followed him in singing the same. There was big gathering. All of a sudden a very big snake came in the middle of the Sangat. The entire gathering began running but Sant Ji continued singing the Divine Hymns in a very calm manner. The snake went close to the place where Sant Ji was sitting and then went away. Sant Ji observed, "It had come to enjoy the singing of the Divine Hymns."

Voice of children is Voice of God

Sant Ji began taking rest in the house of Wazir Singh in the night. Bhag Bhari said, "The noise created by the children must be disturbing you in your meditation." He observed, "The voice of the children is free from ill-will. It is the voice of God. They create noise just before the sunrise. I am not disturbed by it."

Tune the mind with sound

One day, Bhag Bhari submitted, "Sir, when you are engaged in the meditation, each early morning, I churn curd at that time. The sound of churning must be a disturbing factor." He replied, "I tune my mind to this sound. Do not worry."

Rains came in dry season

One year, there were no rains in Kanoha. People were in great trouble. The entire village came to the house of Wazir Singh and requested Sant Ji to plough some field so that rains should fall. Bhag Bhari then went to the cottage followed by all others. She fell at his feet and with folded hands submitted, "The entire village begs the boon of rainfall. Kindly plough one field so that rains may fall." He smiled and observed, "Do you want me suffer in the way the Tappa suffered ?" So saying, he came out. He had hardly put his hand on the plough, when rains fell in torrents.

Shaheeds seen

One night, Bhai Kirpal Singh got up at about 2 a.m. He went towards the water channel. He was astonished to see that five very sturdy and powerful warrior-like Singhs were going on horsebacks towards the grove. Bhai Kirpal Singh, with all respects, bowed before them and enquired as to who they were and where were they going at that time of the night. They replied, "O brother-Sikh, why are you asking this question ?" Bhai Kirpal

Singh came to see Sant Ji in the morning and told this story to him. Sant Ji observed, "You should not talk about this any further to anyone. The Shaheed (Martyr) soldiers of the tenth Satguru roam about in this way. No one should interfere in their program and none should tell anything about them to anyone."

Sant Ji got a Divine Message that the last moments of Bhai Wazir Singh should soon come. He was not then at Kanoha. When he reached Kanoha, he found that Bhai Wazir Singh had very high fever. He took him in his lap and began uttering 'Waheguru'.

Conferring of Salvation on Wazir Singh

Bhai Wazir Singh began repeating the same. In a short time, Bhai Wazir Singh left this world, uttering 'Waheguru' 'Waheguru'. After performing Bhog of Akhand Path (i.e. Continuous Recitation of Sri Guru Granth Sahib from beginning to the end), he came from Kanoha and sat on the sandy ground of Luni. He performed continuous meditation for eight months here.

True Sadhu need not wear coloured clothes

Some true stories of this period are as follows :

One day, a Nirmala Sadhu saw Sant Ji Maharaj sitting on sands at Luni. He was greatly influenced by his spiritual powers and looks. He, with folded hands, submitted, "Sir, coloured robes are the proper dress for a Sadhu. If you permit, I may bring the same." He smiled and replied, "I like the natural colour and not the colour you suggest."

Coarse clothes are proper for True Saints

After sometime, the marriage of the daughter of

Baba Khem Singh was to be performed. He sent food-stuffs and other materials for the free kitchen and shawls for Sant Ji through S. Nirmal Singh, Malik Khazan Singh and Rai Bahadur Buta Singh of Rawalpindi. Sant Ji kept the materials for free kitchen and returned the shawls, after observing, "Shawls look nice for Baba Ji. For Faqirs, like me, the piece of coarse warm cloth is enough." When they went back and told about this to Baba Khem Singh Ji, he observed, "If he continuously wears this *Bhuri* (warm coarse cloth), his reputation will spread everywhere and even Kings will bow before him. He has returned these shawls. A day will come when he will accept these." Again Baba Ji sent more things for the free kitchen. Sant Ji Maharaj directed Langar to be arranged on a wide scale. This was done.

Testing Spiritual Powers is not good

Once Bhai Kanahiya Lal, Bhai Atma Singh Kohli and Bhai Duna Singh thought, "People talk of great penances being performed by Sant Ji Maharaj, so let us see how far is this correct." All three went at night to Luni stealthily and by turn each of them watched Sant Ji Maharaj, who remained continuously absorbed in meditation and worship. They were terrified on account of their sinful thinking and due to their own conduct. They came early morning to beg pardon from Sant Ji. They fell at his feet and humbly submitted, "Sir, we have committed a great sin. We wanted to test your conduct. Kindly excuse us." Sant Ji Maharaj observed, "You are given pardon this time, but in future do not test the genuineness of a True Sadhu. Bhai Atma Singh and Bhai Duna Singh subsequently got themselves baptised with the Nectar of the double-edged sword. Bhai Duna Singh became so much detached from the household affairs that, in due course, he became a Sadhu and engaged himself in the devotional worship and meditation.

No worry for body

One day, Sant Ji after taking bath, began meditation on the sands of Luni. He did not care for his body even. It was noon time. Sant Baj Singh came from Thoha Khalsa to pay respects to him. When he reached there, he was astonished to see him sitting calmly on the burning hot sand, in deep meditation. Drops of perspiration were falling in large numbers on the hot burning sand. Sant Baj Singh bowed before Sant Ji from some distance. He wanted to sit there, but it was so hot that he had not the courage to stay there. He came back and sat under a tree. In the evening, at the time of recitation of Rehras (evening prayers), Sant Ji opened his eyes and Sant Baj Singh paid his respects.

A Dacoit changed into Good Sikh

One devoted Sikh, Bhai Gausha of Kalar, was the follower of Sant Bhim Singh of Thamali. He was a terrible dacoit and the whole surroundings were afraid of him. He used to conceal himself in the thick grove of Luni for a good deal of time, to escape arrest by the police. When he saw Sant Ji Maharaj sitting in meditation day and night on the sands of Luni, his mind became somewhat pure. He was attracted by the spiritual status of Sant Ji. He slowly began coming near him to pay respects. In due course, he talked with him and fell at his feet. He requested for his shelter. He begged pardon for his past misdeeds and sins and became a devoted follower of Sant Ji.

Yag at Luni

At Luni, Sant Ji performed Akhand Path and a big Yag (distribution of free food etc., by holding a free kitchen on a large scale). Then he shifted to Dera Khalsa. Here he, sat in meditation in the thick grove of trees. Sometimes later, Sant Ji Maharaj secretly shifted to Sagri Pind. Here he performed meditation under a banyan tree.

Working as labourers—earn bread and then perform Meditation

When after taking meals at Dera Khalsa, Sant Ji Maharaj came out to take rest, he conferred with his companions and observed, "One can meditate upon God and Satguru in a better way, if he takes food out of his own earned money. Why should we be a burden on others ? We should work as labourers and earn something." On the next day, Bhai Kalyan Singh and one other companion changed their clothes, so as to look like labourers and went to the village to work as such. They worked at four annas per day. A big house of a Sikh money-lender was under construction. They worked so hard that he became suspicious that they were not ordinary labourers. On his enquiry, they asserted that they were labourers. The money-lender said, "You have finished the work of one day in half a day, by your extraordinary honesty." In the evening he wanted to pay eight annas each for this reason, but they refused to accept more than four annas. Both of them then received eight annas in the evening and cooked food out of this earning. Sant Ji was highly pleased to take meals prepared out of the flour etc., purchased by spending eight annas. He said, "This kind of food has a special and pure taste. I will also go with you tomorrow to work as labourer."

On the next day, Sant Ji also changed his dress and went to work as a labourer. When he reached the place, the owner of the house prayed with folded hands, "Sir, I have noticed Divine Luster on your face. You are not a labourer. You are a Godly Saint. Kindly allow us to serve you." Meanwhile almost the whole village collected at the spot and all fell at the feet of Sant Ji and prayed him to shower his grace on them. Sant Ji accepted this request and observed, "You must supply food to me out of honestly earned income." He then went to stay in the hut outside the village and started continuous meditation. He stayed there for two months. As usual, Kirtan in the morning and recitation of Gurbani was the daily routine. Many persons gained spiritual benefits and reformed themselves.

CHAPTER VI

VISITED RAWALPINDI AND OTHER PLACES

Sant Ji subsequently came to Rawalpindi and took abode near a temple. Kirtan of Asa-Di-Var from 4 a.m. to 6.a.m. and then meditation was the daily programme place. From this he shifted to Mooanghat (where dead bodies were burnt). Large number of Sangat flocked to that place and used to bring fruits, etc. The place called 'Tapo Ban' was close by. Here Sadhus used to come. They came to pay respects to Sant Ji Maharaj and were much influenced by his sweet talk.

Visited Ram Kund

From this place Sant Ji Maharaj went to 'Ram Kund', which is nearly six miles away from Rawalpindi. After two days' stay here, he climbed up the hill and stayed there.

Tiger came

At this place, a tiger came twice. Sant Ji woke his companions and observed, "See this tiger. You remain sleeping at this time of early morning; but even animals pray to God at this time." At 'Ram Kund', Bhai Buta Singh Ragi forgot his self while meditating on the Name. Sant Ji Maharaj was pleased at this and observed that one should remain in this state throughout.

Serpents came to hear Divine Music

When Sant Ji Maharaj was residing in the 'gupha' (closed underground hut) near Rawalpindi, four snakes used to come and sit near the place, when Kirtan was performed. Bhai Prem Singh was terrified to see this. But Sant Ji directed Bhai Buta Singh Ragi to continue with the Kirtan and observed, "These cobras are enjoying the Kirtan." At the close of Kirtan, they used to leave the place.

Visit to Haripur

Sant Ji Maharaj left Rawalpindi and went to Haripur via Khanpur. He took abode in the garden outside the city. Here Thakur Nihal Singh used to come to pay respects to Sant Ji. Sant Ji stayed here for one month and Kirtan and recitation of Gurbani were the usual programs in the morning and the evening.

Meeting with Muslim Faqirs who got Spiritual Pleasure

During this period, one day Sant Ji went to another garden, where about forty Muslim Faqirs were residing. They were smoking. They stopped smoking and paid full respects to Sant Ji Maharaj. Sant Ji directed the Ragis to start Kirtan. Sant Ji himself sang this Divine Hymn :

ਯਕ ਅਰਜ ਗੁਫਤਮ ਪੇਸਿ ਤੋ ਦਰ ਗੋਸ ਕੁਨ ਕਰਤਾਰ ॥
ਹਕਾ ਕਬੀਰ ਕਰੀਮ ਤੂ ਬੇਐਬ ਪਰਵਦਗਾਰ ॥੧॥
ਦੂਨੀਆ ਮੁਕਾਮੇ ਫਾਨੀ ਤਹਕੀਕ ਦਿਲ ਦਾਨੀ ॥
ਮਮ ਸਰ ਮੂਇ ਅਜਰਾਈਲ ਗਿਰਫਤਹ ਦਿਲ ਹੇਚਿ ਨ ਦਾਨੀ ॥੧॥ਰਹਾਉ॥
ਜਨ ਪਿਸਰ ਪਦਰ ਬਿਰਾਦਰਾਂ ਕਸ ਨੇਸ ਦਸਤੰਗੀਰ ॥
ਆਖਿਰ ਬਿਅਫਤਮ ਕਸ ਨ ਦਾਰਦ ਚੂੰ ਸਵਦ ਤਕਬੀਰ ॥੨॥
ਸਭ ਰੋਜ ਗਾਸਤਮ ਦਰ ਹਵਾ ਕਰਦੇਮ ਬਦੀ ਖਿਆਲ ॥
ਗਾਹੇ ਨ ਨੇਕੀ ਕਾਰ ਕਰਦਮ ਮਮ ਈ ਚਿਨੀ ਅਹਵਾਲ ॥੩॥
ਬਦਬਖਤ ਹਮ ਚੁ ਬਖੀਲ ਗਾਫਿਲ ਬੇਨਜਰ ਬੇਬਾਕ ॥
ਨਾਨਕ ਬੁਗੋਯਦ ਜਨੁ ਤੁਰਾ ਤੇਰੇ ਚਾਕਰਾਂ ਪਾ ਖਾਕ ॥੪॥੧॥

(ਰਾਗ ਤਿਲੰਗ ਮਹਲਾ ੧, ਪੰਨਾ ੭੨੧)

1. I utter one supplication before you. O, the Creator, give your ear and hear it.
2. You are True, Great, Merciful and Faultless, oh my Charisher.
3. The world is perishable. Know this firmly in your mind.
4. The angel of death, Israel, will catch by the hair (the sinful person), but his mind does not realise this (does not care for it). 1. Pause.
5. The wife, son, father and brothers and none else will hold sinner's hand (in the end), (will not save him from the net of death).
6. At length, when the man falls (dies) and when the death-prayer is to be performed, there shall be none to rescue the sinner. 2.
7. Day and night (the sinner) wanders (spends his life) in greedy ways and in thinking of evil deeds.

8. Never did the sinner, perform virtuous deeds. This is his (pitiable) condition (the way of life). 3.

9. (The sinner) is unfortunate, miserly, negligent, shameless and without fear (of God).

10. (Satguru) Nanak (says) I am your slave and I am the dust of the servants of your slaves. 4.1.

On hearing this, the faqirs were greatly influenced and felt spiritual pleasure. They knelt before Sant Ji and began loudly proclaiming, "O wonderful Allah, you are very great, your Nature is also most wonderful. All men are same in Your kingdom."

Story of Granthi Bachan Singh—Shun the Society of Liquor Vendors etc.

One day, Granthi Bachan Singh, who was following Sant Ji Maharaj, began talking with Hari Singh, who was resident of Choha Khalsa. Hari Singh was a liquor vendor at Haripur. He took Bachan Singh inside his shop and enquired about the welfare of his relations, residing at Choha Khalsa. When Bachan Singh reached the Religious Congregation (Diwan), one person rose and said, "Sant Ji Maharaj, I saw one of your devotees entering the liquor shop. He should be punished." Hari Singh had also come by that time. He explained the whole matter and said, "Granthi Bachan Singh never took liquor. I only enquired about the welfare of my relatives." Sant Ji smiled at this and observed, "Although Bachan Singh had by chance entered the shop, yet the blot on his honour has been the result. I warn all the Sangat to ever shun the society of sinful persons."

Tour of Pothohar—again visited Kanoha

Sant Ji felt that Mata Bhag Bhari and her relatives

had great yearing to see him. So Sant Ji Maharaj went straight to Kanoha from Haripur. When he reached her house, she fell at his feet and wept for a good deal of time, as a token of supreme respect for him. Sant Ji Maharaj then lifted the head of Mata Bhag Bhari and observed, "I have always been with you. My true form is in 'Satguru and Waheguru', Who reside in your heart."

Sant Ji went to Amritsar—Correct way of giving money to the Ragis, explained

When Sant Ji reached 'Dukh Bhanjani' he heard the Ragis singing Divine Hymns. Sangat was giving money from time to time. He observed, "It is better if you give whatever you desire when Kirtan is finished. The Ragis can make prayers for the welfare of the donors at the close of the Kirtan." On this occasion, Sangat from various places, such as Dera Khalsa, Kalar, Thoha, Nara, Choha, Mator, Thamali etc., had gathered to attend the celebrations at 'Dukh Bhanjani'. Sangat from each of these places requested Sant Ji to visit their places and confer Divine Grace on them. Bhai Kashmira Singh and Bhai Sadhu Singh of Kahuta also made similar requests. Sant Ji did not give any reply.

Death Projects the Mortal till the Appointed Time

At 1 a.m., Sant Ji Maharaj took Bhai Kashmira Singh with him and without telling anybody started for Kahuta. It was very hot season. There was a walled spring (Baoli). Sant Ji was warned by Kashmira Singh not to go near it as snakes might be sitting there. He did not care for this and entered this spring and drank water. He observed, "Death (Kaal) protects the man and will not come till the appointed time. Why should you worry ?"

Story of Muslim Faqir—Atmosphere surcharged with the Naam

Sant Ji left Kahuta and started on the road to Punchh. About a mile off he sat at a beautiful spring. From this place at a distance of nearly one and half mile a true Muslim Faqir lived, who ever remained absorbed in the remembrance of God. After Sant Ji began meditation on the spring the Faqir felt that the sound of 'God' 'God' (Waheguru) was coming from the entire hillock. The Faqir was astonished at this and believed that some true devotee of Satguru Nanak Dev must be meditating near about. He yearned to see such a saint. On the next day, Sant Ji went up to take bath in the spring, situated near the cottage of the Faqir, who paid respects to him and came to know about the place where he was sitting. The Faqir brought some parched grams and placed these before Sant Ji, by way of offerings. He took some and observed that this event should not be narrated to anybody. Sant Ji used to go to this Faqir occasionally. The Faqir could not control himself and one day he told the visitors that a true Sikh Saint was sitting near this place and the whole atmosphere was surcharged and was resounding with the Name of Waheguru.

More Stories of the Snakes etc.

During the periods of meditation some extraordinary events occurred :

a) Big Serpent and a small Snake

At Kanoha a very big serpent used to reside near the cottage close to the walled spring and it would visit Sant Ji to pay its respects. A smaller snake used to live in the cottage and used to come and sit near Sant Ji who many times, used to lift it and place it in the niche outside the cottage. Anyone who used to come near the cottage was terrified to see it. It used to hiss at him at that time. But would keep quite, when Sant Ji so ordered it. It served as a watchman.

b) Scorpion came

One day a big scorpion was seen sitting on the body of Sant Ji Maharaj. Devotees cried aloud that it was very poisonous and should be removed. Sant Ji Maharaj observed, "It has come to pay respects. It will itself go of its own accord. It is not necessary to remove it. If God wills, it will sting me otherwise not." Soon scorpion came down and went away.

c) Muslim Dacoits came to attack Sant Ji Maharaj but bowed before Him

Sant Ji narrated a story of his long stay at the cottage in Kanoha. He told that one day four Muslim dacoits, with sharp-edged weapons in their hands, came in the cottage at about 1 a.m. and asked him to give to them whatever he had possessed. Sant Ji said, "I have got this steel pot." The thieves lifted it. Then one of them noticed a brilliant thing on the arm of Sant Ji. He enquired what it was. Sant Ji replied, "This is the steel 'Kara', but I will not part with it. It is dearer to me than my life." The dacoits then said, "This is a Faqir of Allah," so saying they left the place.

d) Baptism by the Double-Edged Sword (Amrit Parchar) on a large scale—Professor Jodh Singh took Amrit

When Sant Ji was at Kahuta, many devotees took Amrit. Bhai Lal Singh, preacher of the Singh Sabha Rawalpindi, Professor Jodh Singh and others became Amrit-dhari Singhs. Professor Jodh Singh aged about

18 years, was at that time working as headmaster of the Khara Middle School, Kahuta. He had then passed F.A. In due course, he became a professor in the Khalsa College, Amritsar and afterwards became the Vice-Chancellor of the Punjabi University at Patiala. Sant Ji Maharaj directed Bhai Lal Singh to work as a preacher without pay, but only maintenance charges should be received by him. He agreed to this. His pay was rupees thirty per month which he received from the Singh Sabha, Rawalpindi. He now used to receive only Rupees ten only per month to maintain himself and his wife. He fulfilled this promise throughout his life. Sant Ji used to live at the walled spring (Baoli) outside the township. He used to hold religious congregations (Diwans) three times each day at the Panchaity Gurdwara. In the morning, Asa Di Var was sung. In the evening from 4 p.m. to 7 p.m., Amrit Parchar, followed by evening prayer, took place. In the night from 8 p.m. to 10 p.m., Katha and History from *Suraj Parkash* was narrated.

e) Story of Bhai Budh Singh (A very old Sikh)

One important story of this period is as follows :

A number of Sikhs of the Ilaqa went to see Bhai Budh Singh aged about 125 years, and sought his advice as to whether they should take Amrit or not. This Bhai Budh Singh was a devoted Sikh. He was in the service of Sodhi Kahan Singh, who was the governor of the Ilaqa, during the regime of Maharaja Ranjit Singh and was present when the Maharaja got Ardas performed to get passage through the flooded river Attock.

Bhai Budh Singh told the visitors that he would give a reply the next day. When the Sikhs again came to consult Bhai Budh Singh, he observed, "I read in Gita that the feet of a true Saint touched the skull of a man, who was carried by Angels to the paradise, after it was changed into a full fledged man. Now is the golden opportunity. This great Saint is administering Amrit with his own hands. Please take it immediately." Bhai Budh Singh was now the first Sikh to take Amrit. After him thousands of men, women and children took Amrit and became Amritdhari Singhs. Sant Ji sang some verses at that time. "Drink Amrit prepared with the double-edged sword. Get benefits of the human birth," was the first verse. The Sangat repeated and sang these verses after Sant Ji sang each verse each time. The melodious and holy song resounded in the atmosphere. The withered souls of the sinful persons became green on hearing these verses. Sant Ji directed each newly-made Singh to repeat 100 to 500 recitation of Jap Ji Sahib.

f) Visit to Dhurma—Sulakhan Singh got a son

Sant Ji then visited Dhurma. Jamadar Sulakhan Singh got a cottage built there for him. One day, the Jamadar requested Sant Ji to confer the boon of a son. Sant Ji observed, "Meditate on the Satguru. Recite Gurbani." He obeyed this direction. In due course, a son was born to him, who was named as Attar Singh. He subsequently became famous as Chaudhari Attar Singh.

g) Amrit given to the dead body of Sital Das

One Sital Das, goldsmith, was anxious to take Amrit, but his mother-in-law did not allow him to leave the house. It so happened that he died suddenly the same night. When Sant Ji came to know in the morning, after the Asa-Di-Var, that this man had left this world without Amrit and that his dead body was being taken to the burning ground, he got prepared Amrit and went to see

41

the dead body. He put some Amrit in the mouth of the dead body of Sital Das and some on his head. Now a very loud sound, like the sound of a bomb-blast was heard, when his skull was burst. Sant Ji observed, "Due to the intense desire of this devotee to take Amrit, which he could not take, his last breathe halted in the Tenth Door of the brain. Due to the Divine Power of the Amrit, when his desire to take it was fulfilled, he left for the Kingdom of Satguru Gobind Singh Ji Maharaj and got Emancipation."

h) Visit to Gurdwara Bhai Joga Singh at Peshawar

After this, Sant Ji Maharaj left for Peshawar and resided at the Gurdwara of Bhai Joga Singh. Here daily congregations were held. Amrit Parchar on a very wide scale took place. Religious discourses were given. Kirtan was performed. One day, Sant Ji came to know that Baba Kahan Singh was a spiritually gifted Saint, who lived close-by. Sant Ji went to see this Saint. As soon as he went to see him, he got up from his cot and paid respects. Sant Ji talked with him about religious matters. Baba Ji said, "I live ever in joy. On seeing you, my pleasure has become immense."

i) Do not talk ill of True Saints, who are not different from God-Visit to Dhan Mangalwal and Chakwal

From Rawalpindi, Sant Ji went to Dhan Mangalwal, without telling anybody. The devotees tried to know where he had gone. After great difficulty they found that he was at Dhan Mangalwal. Here he was lying senseless on a bed. Somebody had mixed mercury in his food, so he became seriously ill. When Sangat came to see him, he got up and said, "I am quite well. All this is the written command of God."

For proper treatment the devotees took him to Chakwal. In a few days he regained his former health. Many Diwans (Religious Functions) were held, Kirtan was performed and Amrit was administered. People flocked to pay respects to Sant Ji.

Visit to Kalar—Meditation in Winter on Sands at Luni

From Chakwal, Sant Ji came to Kalar via Sukhi and Dera Khalsa. At Kalar he took meals at the house of Bhai Ram Singh Kohli. Sant Ji wanted to go to Kanoha. When he was crossing the stream, one man foolishly remarked, "How healthy and stout is this figure. He is shirking earning money by labour." On hearing this, Sant Ji stopped going further and started most difficult and deep meditation throughout the winter, sitting on the sands at Luni.

Visit to Mirpur (Jammu)

From Kalar, Sant Ji went to Mirpur in Jammu State. Here he stayed for one and a half month. Here lived a devoted Bhagat, who was a *Chela* of some Param Hans. He performed rituals of various kinds but did not get peace of mind. He came to pay respects to Sant Ji. One day on seeing Sant Ji, he got a great spiritual joy and calmness. He requested Sant Ji for obtaining permanent peace of mind and submitted, "I have practised customary worship and rituals; but the stone-like mind has not become soft." Sant Ji gave him Gur-Mantar and advised him to meditate on the Satguru and then obtain True Results. He adopted this method and got a great peace of mind.

Scorpion at Bagham

Sant Ji was at Bagham. He was fully absorbed in performing Kirtan. The Sangat and even whole atmosphere became spellbound. A dangerous and big black scorpion appeared there and went up on the back of Sant Ji Maharaj. It roamed there till Kirtan came to an end. Some Sikhs, who had seen it cried loudly, "It will sting Sant Ji Maharaj." Sant Ji Maharaj observed, "It will not cause any harm. It has come to hear Divine Hymns and pay respects." Some time later, it came down itself and went away.

The meaning of Prem (Love) for God and Guru, explained

Sant Ji Maharaj observed :

The word 'Prem' means that the devotee leaves I-am-ness. He leaves his self and gets fully absorbed in the object of love. Such should be the love of the devotee for the Satguru. Such love attracts the attention of the beloved automatically, without using any words or outwardly ways of communication. The Satguru, then comes to the assistance of the true devotee.

News of Forcibly Cutting the Long Hair of some Sikhs at Jalandhar—Roots of the Khalsa cannot be destroyed by anyone.

One day, a young devotee named Hukam Singh read a most tragic news in the paper that some mischievous persons had forcibly cut the long hair of some Sikhs at Jalandhar and had made ropes of the same and sold the same in the bazar. The young boy began weeping after reading this news and wanted to convey it to Sant Ji at the earliest opportunity. After some days, he came to know that Sant Ji had come to Kanoha. He immediately went to Kanoha. Sant Ji was in deep meditation in the cottage in the grove. He fell at the feet of Sant Ji and paid respects. Hukam Singh took the paper from his pocket and read it out, wept and said, "How big is the act of cruelty. Will sometimes come when we will get the upper hand."

A special glare appeared on the face of Sant Ji and he observed, "Who can uproot the roots of the Sikhs and the Khalsa ? None can do this. These roots have gone deep in the nether regions. Many came and tried to efface the Sikhs. Many will come in future to do so. But they have all miserably failed and will certainly fail in the future. But the 'drama' (the mission) will be completely fulfilled. Remember the ever true words of the Satguru Gobind Singh Ji that the Khalsa will spread in whole of the world."

Pujaris became envious

He again came to Amrtisar. The 'Pujaris' of Darbar Sahib became envious of Sant Ji. One day, when the Jatha of Sant Ji was performing Kirtan, Bhai Bur Singh used harsh and unsuitable words for Sant Ji, who however, remained perfectly calm. Sant Ji got up and came in front of the Bunga of Sohals, where he started Kirtan and the Sangat gathered there. The Pujaris now realised their mistake. They came and begged pardon from Sant Ji, who observed, "I am the dog of Satguru Nanak Dev Ji. If somebody loves me, I go near him, otherwise I go far away from him." The Sangat also felt aggrieved on this occasion and their respect for Sant Ji increased manifold.

He used to rub His forehead at the Main Gate of Darbar Sahib for a long time

After the Diwan used to end, Sant Ji used to go to Darbar Sahib and used to rub his forehead, after bowing it, on the floor, for a good deal of time. A big black spot appeared on the forehead, for this reason. One day, Giani Thakur Singh came to pay respects to Sant Ji and saw him rubbing his forehead and enquired the reasons for this. Tears rolled down and in this state Sant Ji replied, "Giani Ji, when I pass around the Darbar Sahib then many Sikhs bow before me (an insignificant worm). I offer this debt and pay it to the Satguru."

Tour of Amritsar district—Give Amrit to ladies, prepared by Double-edged Sword

Now a large number of people of the villages etc., also began coming to see and pay respects to Sant Ji. On their request, Sant Ji toured the rural areas of Amritsar. Amrit began to be administered on a very large scale. Sant Ji ordered that the Amrit prepared with double-edged sword instead of prepared with a sword (Kirpan) should also be given to women. He said, "The difference between men and women is not warranted by Sikh Religion."

The man who cuts his hair pricks the body of the Satguru

At Tarn Taran, Sant Ji used to hold Diwans at the Bunga of Mata Ram Kaur. Amrit was being administered daily on a large scale. One day, a Sikh stood up in the congregation and with folded hands requested Sant Ji, "Kindly pardon me. I have removed some of my hair. My mind has lost all peace since then." Sant Ji closed his eyes and tears rolled down. He was shocked to hear this and observed in an emotional voice, "Have you not read the verses of Bhai Gurdas Ji and verses of Gurbani, which proclaims that in each hair live all the gods, nay, even God himself lives there ? By pulling up your hair you have pricked the body of the Satguru." How can you remain peaceful ? Now make a solemn promise that you will not disobey any other mandate also. They, who spend their lives without infringing the Divine Commands, get Supreme Spiritual Joy and Permanent Place."

Master Tara Singh given Amrit—Big Diwans held

In due course, Sant Ji again visited Dera Khalsa. Throughout the Pothohar this news reached all. Sangats from Kallar, Kanoha, Gujar Khan, Sagri, Rawat, Rawalpindi and other places flocked to pay respects to Sant Ji. Amrit Parchar took place each day on a large scale. One day, Bhai Mohan Singh Rahi, Bhai Teja Singh Mangat, Bhai Jagat Singh Pardesi and Chaudhari Kartar Singh started together to pay respects to Sant Ji. In the way, they decided to test his spiritual powers. They decided that if he could read their minds they would recognize him as a True Saint and would take Amrit from him. On reaching Dera Khalsa, they went inside the cottage, where Sant Ji was sitting, and sat down after formal salutations. Sant Ji observed, "Bhai Sahib, what consultations took place between you ? I am not a Saint, I am the humble slave of Satguru Nanak Dev Ji, who alone can read others' minds. However, when he showers the powers of communication with others these are conferred on his humble servants (dogs)." They were now satisfied on hearing all this and fell at the feet of

47

Sant Ji. They took Amrit on the next day. In those days about sixty Sadhus had gathered there. They had different creeds. Bhai Mohan Singh Rahi asked the reasons for collecting them. Sant Ji said, "They serve as the fence around me." Master Tara Singh Ji, Sant Teja Singh Ji, Granthi of Nankana Sahib. also took Amrit at Dera Khalsa.

Now True Guru is Guru Granth Sahib only

At Dera Khalsa, Sikhs used to come even from long distances and were given Amrit. Sant Ji Maharaj used to tell all that the true Guru is Sri Guru Granth Sahib which is the embodiment of the Ten Satgurus and used to teach the way of respecting the Guru Granth Sahib. He would assert that he was a mere slave of the Satguru.

Tenth Satguru showers the Nectar of the Name when Amrit is given

One day, a Sikh came to the place and requested Sant Ji Maharaj that he should himself administer the Amrit. Sant Ji Maharaj replied, "Five of my companions will prepare the Amrit. When the Five Piaras appear before Sri Guru Granth Sahib and repeat the prescribed Banis (Divine Hymns) while preparing Amrit, the Tenth Satguru Himself showers the Nectar of the Name. The Nectar infuses bravery and spiritual love. The Tenth Satguru himself sits there and himself administers the Amrit. Please leave all baseless doubts." On hearing this, he begged pardon and requested that the Panj Piaras might kindly prepare and administer the Amrit to him. This was done.

A member of the Singh Sabha used improper language—Shabad-Guru is the Incarnation of God

Once a member of the Singh Sabha Rawalpindi came to see Sant Ji. Devoted Sikhs were bowing before him. That member of the Singh Sabha did not like this and while giving a lecture, used derogatory language against Sant Ji, who remained calm and quiet. When he finished his speech, Sant Ji called him and seated him close to himself. Sant Ji then addressed the Sangat and observed, "Brothren, never bow your head before me. Shabad-Guru is the Incarnation of God in this dark age. All shall have to bow their heads before Sri Guru Granth Sahib."

He never sat on cushion—Adopt Virtues, leave arguments

Sant Ji never sat on a cushion in the presence of Sri Guru Granth Sahib. Even in the evening Diwans, when Sri Guru Granth Sahib was not present, he would sit on a *duree* spread for all. In the evening sittings first Katha and history was narrated. Sant Ji used to observe, "Let us adopt some virtue. This is better than hearing many discourses."

Biggest virtue is to excuse others

Giani Sunder Singh and one other Sikh asked Sant Ji, "What virtue should be adopted ?" Sant Ji observed, "The biggest virtue is to excuse and pardon others. To tolerate the harsh words of others is equal to the greatest penance and the biggest virtue."

Sanyasi (Parm Hans) took Amrit

One day, Giani Sunder Singh, who was much influenced by the new Singh Sabha movement, asked a

Sanyasi (Parm Hans) who had come there, not to remove his hair and keep them as given by the nature. The Sanyasi became very angry and said, "These are my crops (property). I may cut these or keep them, as desired by me. What to you ?" The poor soul forgot the owner of the field i.e. God. In the evening sitting, Sant Ji came out of his cottage. The Sikhs and many Sadhus were also sitting there. Bhai Kalyan Singh requested the Sanyasi (Parm Hans) to come and take a seat. His anger had not, as yet, subsided. He said, "I do not want to sit near you, dog." On hearing this, Sant Ji with great calmness and love said, "Sanyasi Ji, I am your dog. Please come and grace us." On hearing these sweet words, which had a magical influence on the Sanyasi, he came forward and fell at the feet of Sant Ji Maharaj and observed, "You are the physical form of Satguru Gobind Singh Ji." Sant Ji said, "None has ever been or will ever be like Satguru Gobind Singh Ji. I am his humble servant." He prayed, "Kindly give the Amrit and make me Singh." This was complied with.

True Way of preaching Sikh Religion explained

Sant Ji remained at Dera Khalsa for two months. Before Sant Ji Maharaj came, the spiritual condition of Pothohar was miserable. There were no true preaching of the Sikh Religion. None followed the mandates of the Gurbani. Congregations were held on the eighth day i.e. each Sunday. Lot of time was wasted in giving empty speeches. People did not like sincere singing of Divine Hymns. Due to the great spiritual influence of meditation of the Name, true worship of the Satgurus and Gurbani, the dry and dead waves were converted into green spiritual joy and peace by the grace of Sant Ji. Many times he used to say, "I am taking baths in the living ocean of the Nectar of the Name."

CHAPTER VII

VISITED LAHORE AND SINDH AND OTHER PLACES

Propagation of the Sikh Religion in Lahore

From Dera Khalsa, Sant Ji Maharaj came to Lahore where he stayed for about a month. Thousands of devotees, men, women and children took Amrit. S. Mehar Singh Chawla, S. Harnam Singh Atewala and Bhai Jawahar Singh and many other prominent Sardars became Singhs.

Do not believe in caste-system, Giani Dit Singh's story

One day, the evening Diwan was held at the birth-place of Guru Ram Dass (The Gurdwara) in Chuna Mandi, Lahore. Bhai Dit Singh spoke on the Sikh Religion and the greatness of the Satgurus. Sant Ji was highly pleased to hear this speech. After Giani Dit Singh finished his speech, he bowed before Sri Guru Granth Sahib and wanted to leave the congregation but Sant Ji called him and gave him a seat near himself and told him to first get Karah Parshad and then go. Giani Dit Singh submitted, "Sir, if I remain sitting in the Sangat, they will not accept Karah Parshad, because they think that I belong to a low caste." Sant Ji Maharaj felt it very much and spoke loudly, "O Satguru Gobind Singh Ji, how long will your beloved Sikhs be disgraced like this?" He stressed that it was a great sin to believe in caste-system.

Tour of the Sindh

Sant Ji left Lahore and started for Sindh. He did not take any foodstuffs etc., with him for use in the journey;

51

nor did he inform anyone about his tour. Sant Ji had prohibited all from taking anything even from the vendors at the Railway Station. For Four days, Sant Ji and his companions remained without food. During the journey, the usual program of singing Asa-Di-Var in the morning and recitation of Gurbani continued even in the train. However, the companions of Sant Ji became extremely hungry and felt weak. But there was no change in the body or face of Sant Ji who remained as happy as ever. Due to the condition of his companions, Sant Ji asked them to get down at Sakhar Railway Station. They then went straight to Sadh Bela Ghat, situated in the Sindh river by boats. On the next day, Sant Ji rose for prayers, as usual at 1 a.m., but all others except Bhai Kalyan Singh continued sleeping. Sant Ji took bath in the river and sat in deep meditation. The companions of Sant Ji did not get up even at 5 a.m. At length, Sant Ji himself called them to get up and to join in the singing of Asa-Di-Var. They woke after a good difficulty. Sant Ji called all of them and told them to first hear him and then go for taking bath.

To become a True Faqir is most difficult

He observed, "Dear Sikhs, to spend one's life as a Faqir is most difficult. The status of a Faqir cannot be acquired till one is fully engaged in Simran (remembrance and worship of God and the Satguru) and performs service, as prescribed by the Gurbani and then forgets his body and his soul realises the Supreme Soul. The importance of wearing the clothes of a Faqir is to at least obey the Divine Orders and to maintain the honour of the status of a Faqir."

Gold is like Yellow Mud for a True Saint

When Sant Ji was at Hyderabad, he was taken by S. Gian Singh to his house. He served food with affection to Sant Ji and his Jatha. He then brought a tray full of sovereigns, covered by cardamoms. Sant Ji Maharaj took the tray. When he began distributing the cardamoms, he noticed sovereigns concealed underneath. Then he observed, "The tray was heavy, because it contained sovereigns. These are mere yellow mud pieces. The Saints, sometimes, are duped by it and they become the slave of mammon (maya). These are of no use to me. The affectionate Sikhs provide food and clothes to us and also purchase tickets for our travel. Why should we keep these sovereigns, with us?" On hearing these Divine Sermons, the Jatha began reciting some relevant verses of Sukhmani Sahib.

Sant Ji Maharaj went to Karachi—Old Lady Prayed for a Son

In due course, Sant Ji Maharaj left Hyderabad and went to Karachi. He showed his grace there and held religious congregations as usual. One day, he went to Manora. A devoted lady paid respects and served the Jatha sincerely. She requested Sant Ji Maharaj, "I have no son. Kindly pray, so that I may get a son." Sant Ji Maharaj observed, "Why do you want to defile your hands with the urine etc., of a child. Remember God and the Satguru. You will get a grown up son." After few days, the lady adopted a child, who served her and her husband and family members, even better than a natural son.

Prophecy about Bhai Amolak Singh who was shot down by a British Sepoy

On the next day, Sant Ji told Bhai Gulab Singh, "Tomorrow at 2 a.m., Bhai Amolak Singh who has a strong desire to pay respects at Hazur Sahib Gurdwara, at Nander, will be shot dead. The Tenth Satguru will take him in his lap. This is the secret Will of the Satguru." Bhai Amolak Singh used to prepare steel Karas (bangles) and Kirpans for use of the Sikhs, who had to take Amrit. The next day, Bhai Amolak Singh went towards the side of the sea at about 2 a.m. He was absorbed in Simran and did not hear the words of a British soldier stationed at the fort, who said, "Who comes there ?" Bhai Amolak Singh did not even understand these words. He went on proceeding further. All of a sudden, the gunshot was heard, which pierced his chest. He died and reached the Kingdom of the Tenth Satguru. At the time of sunrise, after the Asa-Di-Var, some Sadhus conveyed the news to Sant Ji. He observed, "Perform the last rites calmly. No complaint should be made to anybody. The Satguru himself knows all this. Bhai Amolak Singh is a martyr. His services are accepted by the Satguru."

After this event, Sant Ji Maharaj decided to visit and pay respect at Gurdwara Sri Hazur Sahib. Bhai Gola Singh Sindhi and his family members also requested Sant Ji Maharaj to take them there. Many more and some Sadhus also wanted to accompany Sant Ji Maharaj. In all they were about sixty.

Refusal to travel by sea

One Sindhi Sikh requested Sant Ji to go by sea. Sant Ji replied, "We are ordered by the Satguru not to go by ship but only by train." However, on the requests of the

Sindhis, Sant Ji boarded the ship. The ship had hardly gone about two miles from the shore, when it, all of a sudden, stopped moving further and jolted. The Sangat became panicky and prayed to Sant Ji, "We are sorry. We have disobeyed your wish, kindly save us." Sant Ji prayed to Satguru and remained silent for some time. Then he lifted his right hand and the ship became steady. It started backwards and reached the shore. Then Sri Guru Granth Sahib was taken with great respect and pomp and show by the Sangat to the city. Now Sant Ji and others went to Hyderabad Via Marwar, Jaipur etc. and reached Manmad. On reaching Hazur Sahib, thousands of Sikhs gathered at the Railway Station. They wanted to bow before Sant Ji, who observed, "Dear Sikhs, I am a poor Sikh. Let us all bow before the Tenth Satguru." The entire Sangat were full of emotions and were in tears.

The Tenth Satguru seen

One day, Sant Ji was sitting on the bank of river Godavari, at Hazur Sahib. Many Sikhs were also present there. Bhai Hira Singh Ragi, enquired, "Can the Tenth Satguru be seen ?" Sant Ji observed, "Satguru is always with us. The difficulty arises when people have no faith in this truth and their fickle mind is not pure and free from sinful thoughts. The Satguru can be realised by sincere Sikhs." After this, Sant Ji Maharaj sat in perfect meditation and his mind was fixed on the Tenth Master. Bhai Hira Singh had left the place. After some time, the Sangat saw a Supernatural Light of the Mysterious Lightning and the Tenth Satguru was seen, sitting on the blue horse accompanied by the Five Beloved, who were also sitting on their horses. They were seen coming by the Sangat and disappeared in the twinkling of an eye.

The Sangat was pleased as well astonished to see this. When Bhai Hira Singh came back, he heard the whole story. He was sorry, as he had left the place after asking the question.

Never remove 'Kachhera' from both the legs

One day, Bhai Gulab Singh of Amritsar put off his 'Kachhera' and became naked and then jumped into the river Godavari. When he came out, he put on the 'Kachhera'. When in the afternoon Sant Ji wanted to go for a walk, Bhai Gulab Singh extended his hand and wanted to hold the iron vessel for Sant Ji's use. Sant Ji became red with anger and said, "You have committed an offence against the Religion. As you have removed your 'Kachhera' and became naked. One of the most mandatory commands of Satguru Gobind Singh has been disobeyed by you. I will not take water from you. Satguru loves the observance of his Commands and not to human body made of flesh and full of filth." On hearing this, Bhai Gulab Singh fell at the feet of Sant Ji Maharaj and begged pardon. Sant Ji ordered him to wipe the shoes of the Sangat for twenty-five days so that his sin might be wiped off. He followed this and gladly accepted the punishment.

Sant Ji Maharaj left Hazur Sahib for Delhi

One day, when Sant Ji had to leave Hazur Sahib, the Sangat flocked to pay their respects to him. There were surging crowds of Gursikhs and devotees at the Railway Station. They came to bid farewell and were in due grief due to the separation. Sant Ji consoled them and observed, "You must reside here and serve the Tenth Satguru, under whose protection you are passing your days. Kindly ever pray to the Satguru that we may never leave his Lotus Feet and we may never swerve from the true path of true Sikh Religion. Pray that we may go on serving the great Panth and the great Religion till our last breath." The Sangat was in tears and their emotional affection as well as pangs of separation were extremely great.

Chapter VIII

STAY AT DELHI—THEN WENT TO TARN TARAN AND DAMDAMA SAHIB

Sant Ji got down at Manmad and then got another train and reached Delhi. From the railway station he went straight to Gurdwara Sahib Sis Ganj to pay his respects and to rub its dust on his forehead. Then he stayed there, but went to all Historical Gurdwaras and performed Kirtan and held Diwans there. Large number of persons, men, women and children took Amrit. For many days, Sant Ji performed Kirtan on the bank of river Jamuna. Many Pandits and Pujaris attended these and some of them began meditation upon the worship of the Name, as directed by Sant Ji.

Amrit cannot be purchased with money

Once at Tarn Taran Gurdwara, two or three Pujaris made a request to Sant Ji Maharaj to get one and a quarter rupees from each of the Sikhs, who took Amrit, for the

Treasury of the Satguru. Sant Ji Maharaj observed, "Amrit is a priceless Divine Gift. Even the price of all the universes cannot be the consideration for Amrit. This can be obtained by offering one's head. We cannot proclaim that its price is rupees one and a quarter. However, everyone is free to offer his body, mind and wealth to the Satguru."

Visit to Damdama Sahib and other places

From Tarn Taran, Sant Ji Maharaj went to Damdama Sahib to attend the Baisakhi Gurpurab. In the way, he paid respects at Lakhi Jangal.

Sant Ji went to see his sister, Bibi Rattan Kaur at Jawaharke

From Damdama Sahib, Sant Ji reached Jawaharke, where his sister Bibi Rattan Kaur lived, who had as usual came out from her house at about 6 a.m. She was astonished to see a man, standing outside, wearing a small wollen turban. He had a small black blanket on his shoulder. First, she could not recognise him, as she had not seen Sant Ji Maharaj for some years. She then recognised him and embraced him. Sant Ji Maharaj touched her feet and went inside her house. He observed, "Today in the early morning, I desired to meet you and realised that you were remembering me. My attachment with you is just as Satguru Nanak Dev Ji loved his elder sister, Bibi Nanaki." Then Bibi Rattan Kaur prepared meals for her brother, who went on reading from the Janam Sakhi of Bhai Bala the story of Bibi Nanaki, while preparing food for her brother Satguru Nanak Dev Ji.

Sant Ji went to Cheema

Afterwards, Sant Ji visited village Cheema and paid respects to his mother. On the next day, he was to leave the village. Before doing so he went out and sat near the place, where Nanaksar now exists. The mother brought food for him at about noon, which he took with affection. Sant Ji gave her a small portrait of Satguru Nanak Dev Ji.

Sant Ji again went to Dera Khalsa

Sant Ji then went to Dera Khalsa. Nearly one month after his arrival there, he came to know that his mother Mata Bholi had come to Tarn Taran with one of his devotees. Sant Ji sent a 'sewak' to bring her at Dera Khalsa. This was complied with. When she reached there, the evening Diwan was being held outside the cottage of Sant Ji. As usual (at the time of evening Diwans) Sri Guru Granth Sahib was not present. Sant Ji saw her from a distance. He stood up and fell at her feet. Then he smiled and enquired, "Mother, am I doing a bad work ?" The mother observed, "No, No." She stayed there for some days. One day, Mata Bholi told Sant Ji that she wanted to go back to village Cheema. Sant Ji observed, "Do you again want to enter the hole of the mouse ? (i.e. do you want again to entangle yourself in the worldly affairs ?) Stay here, in the society of the True Devotees and prepare yourself to go to the True Home of the Supreme Being." Mata Ji agreed to this. She lived at Dera Khalsa for seven years. However, during this period, sometimes, she would go to Rawalpindi, Kaler and Kanoha, as requested by the devotees.

The Divine Watchmen

After the arrival of Mata Bholi Ji, Sant Ji stayed for one month more at Dera Khalsa. One day, Giani Sunder Singh was sitting near the bed of Sant Ji. He was amazed to see that some fully armed and very built brave Singhs in blue dresses, were standing around Sant Ji's bed, as watchmen. When Sant Ji Maharaj got up, Giani Sunder Singh wanted to know who those figures were. Sant Ji replied, "Bhai Sunder Singh, this Supernatural Divine Vigil remains around a true saint, who, having abandoned his ego, has surrendered his body, mind and wealth and everything to the Satguru." Giani Ji then wanted to know whether these Sikhs afforded protection to the Saints. The reply of Sant Ji Maharaj was, "Yes, but if an impostor says something and does the reverse of it, then they warn him of the evil consequences."

Giani Sunder Singh also saw similar Divine Watchmen around Sant Ji, when he went to attend very big Diwans arranged by the Rawalpindi Singh Sabha.

Sant Ji again visited Hardwar

Sant Ji visited Hardwar on the occasion of Half Kumbh Mela. He stayed at Kankhal and resided in the cottage, meant for detached Saints.

Pandit Ishar Singh was there in those days. Evening and morning Kirtan was performed there. Sant Ji used to sing in prescribed and appropriate measures, the Divine Hymns. Sadhus and students enjoyed this spiritual food. Sant Ji used to pay great respect to Pandit Ishar Singh and used to seat him close to him. Many other Sadhus felt envious. However, Pandit Ishar Singh would proclaim that Sant Ji's reputation would go on increasing and that he would reform the whole world.

Visit to Anandpur Sahib

From Hardwar, Sant Ji came to Anandpur Sahib. He used to go to the bank of river Satluj, after taking breakfast. Bhai Jiva Singh of Nankana Sahib, aged about 24 years, had a yearning to leave the worldly affairs totally. He had also come to Anandpur Sahib in those days. He came to pay respects to Sant Ji also. On enquiry, he was told, "Sant Ji Maharaj was standing there. You may see him." When he came near Sant Ji, he fell at his feet. Sant Ji said, "See that side of the river at the ferry. You come there, I will also reach there." This was complied with. When Sant Ji reached that place he took bath in the river, by diving in it. Sant Ji asked Bhai Jiva Singh, "Have you ever taken a bath in this river ?" His reply was in the negative.

Sant Ji observed, "Tenth Satguru used to take bath in it. You may also dive in it." He obeyed this direction. Then Sant Ji and Bhai Jiva Singh sat under a tree and spread their hairs, which had become wet. Sant Ji Maharaj talked with Bhai Jiva Singh after directing his Sevadar Bhai Ishar Singh to go far away from them. Sant Ji enquired, "Bhai Jiva Singh, have you seen something ? See that the Tenth Master is floating away the big boat (raft) full of Sikhs." Bhai Jiva Singh tried to see this. He kept quiet. Sant Ji Maharaj again made the same observation. On this, Bhai Jiva Singh said, "Sir, I am an ordinary human being. I have not got that Divine Vision, which can enable me to see the Satguru, just as Bhai Dalla, at Damdama Sahib, could not see the canals, mango trees etc., and his eyes could see only sand and wild growth, although the Tenth Satguru wanted him to see the former. Similarly I cannot see the raft and the Satguru. Kindly confer upon me that Divine Vision, so that I may see what you are seeing." Sant Ji was pleased to hear this and observed, "Please keep patience. The Spiritual Vision will dawn upon you." Hardly had Sant Ji said this, when Bhai Jiva Singh saw sailors bringing the raft in which the Tenth Satguru was sitting. The verse that (you will not again obtain the Jewel of human birth, so you make humble prayers now) was sung in Divine tunes and could be heard there.

"Bibek Budh"—(The faculty of distinguishing Evil from Good explained)

"Day and night give your thought to the ways of purest wisdom." On enquiry as to what the exact meaning of the verse was, Sant Ji Maharaj explained, "Not a trace of enmity or hatred should be left in the mind, which should never be inimical towards anyone."

On the Touchstone of Truth only a few will succeed

Sant Ji Maharaj left Mananwala for Mastuana, with a firm determination to complete the works at that place as soon as possible. After staying at the grove of Mastuana, Sant Ji Maharaj started morning and evening Diwans.

CHAPTER IX

VISIT TO PESHAWAR, KOHAT ETC.
AND OTHER STORIES

The next day, Sant Ji wanted to go to Peshawar. He first went to Amritsar and after paying respects there, he along with his Jatha reached Peshawar and stayed there in the Gurdwara of Bhai Joga Singh Ji.

The method of Collecting Money for the Gurdwara Mastuana—No Appeal

He, as usual, performed Kirtan in a most spiritual mood and atmosphere. Even stone-hearted people tried to adopt the True Ways of the Sikh Religion. Out of those, who used to come nearer to Sant Ji to pay respects, he would tell some selected ones to take part in the construction work of Mastuana Sahib. These Sikhs thought themselves to be blessed ones and would pay good amounts and would also collect money from their friends. Sant Ji has disallowed appeal for the funds in Diwans. He used to observe, "Such appeals are the results of ill effects of mammon and not proper at all."

Sant Ji Maharaj was Worshipped as "The Light of God" by Pathans—Visit to Kohat

Sant Ji Maharaj along with his Jatha, went from Peshawar to Kohat. There was scarcity of water in this dry and barren part of the frontier. In that particular year, there were no rains at all. In the way Sant Ji was approached by Pathans who requested, "Sir, you are a True Faqir. Kindly get rains for us. You are yourself the Light of Allah. We see no difference between you and Allah. We are in great trouble, kindly help us." On hearing their woeful story, Sant Ji stayed in the village for the night. The Pathans got food for Sant Ji prepared from the families of Hindu residents of the village. Kirtan was started by Sant Ji. The villagers flocked the place. The waves of Spiritualism spread on all sides. All of a sudden, clouds were seen coming in the sky. Evening prayers were recited. As soon as the Ardas (final prayer) was performed by all standing respectfully before the Creator, it began raining very heavily. The entire tract was flooded with rain waters. The Pathans fell at the feet of Sant Ji Maharaj and submitted, "Sir, you are a perfect Faqir. There is no difference between you and God. We have been saved by you."

Maharaja Hira Singh's son came to pay respects

Once, Sant Ji visited Haripur, from where he came to Rawalpindi and stayed in the house of Malik Mohan Singh. In those days, Tikka Ripuduman Singh, while on his way to Kashmir, came to Rawalpindi. When he came to know about Sant Ji, he went to pay respects. He was so much influenced that he attended the Diwans (evening and morning) for many days. In the morning, Katha of Sri Guru Granth Sahib was performed by Sant Teja Singh of Nankana Sahib. One day Tikka Sahib requested Sant Ji Maharaj to uplift the Malwa side. Sant Ji Maharaj observed, "I am establishing a University and a Gurdwara etc., at the central place in Malwa." Tikka Sahib submitted that he would offer monetary contributions for this purpose.

Saihajdharis (Sikhs without long hair) took Khande-Da-Amrit

In those days, S. Sewa Ram Singh, his father Gurdas and his brother Gobind Dass took Khande-Da-Amrit. Name of S. Sewa Ram Singh previously was Sewa Ram. His father was Naib Tehsildar. Twice before the advice of Sant Ji Maharaj, given to S. Sewa Ram Singh to take Amrit was not accepted by him. But this time he agreed to become a 'Singh'. On that very day, Amrit was prepared for forty persons, fifteen out of whom were 'Saihajdharis'. Then S. Sewa Ram Singh delivered a speech on the topic of Amrit as directed by Sant Ji. He spoke for about forty minutes. It was due to the kindness of Sant Ji that he spoke very well on the subject.

Old man leaves smoking—Took Amrit

Once Sant Ji Maharaj came to Dera Khalsa from Mastuana. When he wanted to go back, he wished to visit Tarn Taran. In the way falls the Railway Station of Aminabad. Here an old man was smoking a 'Hukka' (smoking pipe). One of the followers of Sant Ji requested him not to smoke; but he avoided a reply. Then Sant Ji politely said, "What is the use of smoking ?" These words had a magical effect on him. He, with folded hands, requested Sant Ji, "Kindly visit my village. I will abandon smoking and will become a Sikh." Sant Ji's heart became soft for him. He got down at the Railway Station and went to his village Dhalanwali. The well of this old man was on the roadside. Sant Ji decided to stay there. The old man went to his village and brought three beds and beddings. The followers of Sant Ji said, "Only one is needed. We will take rest on the ground at the feet of Sant Ji." However, Sant Ji Maharaj observed, "I want that all three of us should use beds." The old man left smoking that very day and threw away the 'hukka'. He then visited Gujranwala and took Khande-Da-Amrit and became a Singh. Many more villagers of his place followed him.

Visit to Hyderabad (Sindh) and Karachi where he stayed for three months

In due course, Sant Ji again went to Hyderabad (Sindh). The Sangat showed a great affection and respect for him, who said to his companions, "The Sangat has shown a great regard for us. Let us try their sincerity and request them to give money for the projects of Mastuana Sahib." This was complied with. The Sangat collected Rupees twenty-nine thousand, which amount was sent to Gur Sagar Sahib, Mastuana. One day, Sant Ji left Hyderabad without telling anybody. The Sangat of Hyderabad were yet collecting money for the noble cause. Sant Ji reached Karachi. The affection of Sangat was so great that Sant Ji stayed for three months there. Big amounts were collected there also.

Story of Bhai Sahib Dass—Satguru likes services of the Sangat and not of few rich persons

Bhai Sahib Dass a perfect Sadhu, who remained intoxicated with spiritualism, lived in Sangrur. He used to bring his devotees to pay respects to Sant Ji many times and would say to them, "Let us have the Sight of Thakar Ji." He used to call Sant Ji as 'Thakar Ji'. He used to stand with respect for an hour or so in front of Sant Ji and would go on seeing him with love. Although, Sant Ji used to request him to sit down, yet he would prefer to stand. One day, when Sant Ji Maharaj had finished Kirtan, Bhai Sahib Dass submitted, "Thakar Ji, I want to make a request, if you allow me I my narrate it." Sant Ji Maharaj replied, "Please do command me. What can I do for you ?" Bhai Sahib Dass then observed, "You are collecting money from others for the Gurdwara Sahib. I know that there is a concealed treasure of seven kings burried in the earth. Kindly do not appeal for funds. I will tell you where the treasure is." Sant Ji Maharaj smiled and observed, "All the treasures of the world belong to us but I want to get the service of the Satguru performed by the Sangat with body, mind and wealth."

The prisoner directed to be released

One day, a Policeman of Nabha State was taking a prisoner under arrest. He passed near the Diwan, held by Sant Ji as usual in Mastuana. On hearing the Shabads, the Policeman with the accused sat in the Diwan. Sant Ji looked at these persons and he took pity on the prisoner and said to the Policeman, "Liberate this prisoner. Even the angel of death dare not take any person with him from this place." The Policeman answered, "Sir, I can liberate him, but I shall be punished by the government for doing so." Sant Ji then observed, "You release him. I shall be responsible for the consequences."

The Policeman complied with his direction. As soon as the prisoner was released, a revolution came in his life. He took a basket and began doing manual service at the place where construction work of the Gurdwara was going on. He also collected wood-fuel for the Kitchen. The Policeman stayed there for the day and he took part in doing the holy work for the construction. He went to Nabha on the second day. When the turn of hearing of the case of the said prisoner came, he was called. The Policeman narrated the whole story to Maharaja Hira Singh, who smiled at this and took no further action in the matter. One day Sant Ji all of a sudden started for Lahore by train with a Sewadar to get a life-convict released. Sant Ji got down at the Lahore Railway Station and went in a taxi to the Central Jail, Lahore. Sant Ji said to the sepoy on duty, "I want to see Rehmat Khan, cendemned prisoner, who has been ordered to be hanged after three hours. He has called me." Sant Ji was allowed to go to the condemned cell. On reaching the cell he saw Rehmat Khan in fetters and handcuffs. He was very sincerely praying, "O Satguru Nanak, I am innocent. I shall be hanged without any offence. You are my Proctector. Kindly save me." When he lifted his face, he saw Sant Ji, standing before him and submitted, "Blessed is Satguru Nanak. Blessed is Sant Attar Singh Ji. Sir, I am innocent man who is going to be hanged. Kindly get me liberated." Sant Ji observed, "If you are innocent, you will be released within one hour." After saying this, Sant Ji went outside the Jail. Hardly half an hour had passed, when the telegram from the office of the Governor, before whom Rehmat Khan had given an application for mercy, reached the Jail. In this it was ordered that Rehmat Khan should be immediately released. Sant Ji returned to the Railway Station and Rehmat Khan went to his house. He then brought a shawl and Rupees five hundred as a humble offering to Sant Ji.

Bread with Pickles became most tasteful in the Free Kitchen

Once Giani Sunder Singh of Gujranwala came to Gurdwara Sahib. Bhai Lal Singh, Parcharak (missionary) of Chief Khalsa Diwan, also came there. Sant Ji observed, "This project has been started so that the Malwa Region may also have a centre of education and means of spreading the Sikh Religion. This part of the country is very backward and illiterate. Before these gentlemen took leave to go, Sant Ji Maharaj directed them to eat meals from the Free Kitchen. In those days, very simple food used to be served. It consisted of thick loaves of bread and some pickle only. Sant Ji Maharaj observed, "We want money for the Gurdwara Sahib and so we do not serve (Karah Parshad). Many Sikhs who had come here for doing service have left and only a few remain here, because no dainty foods could be supplied to them. Both Giani Sunder Singh Ji and Giani Lal Singh Ji relished the food of the Langar and submitted, "We have not eaten so tasty food uptil now." This was a miracle in itself.

Most serious Earthquake of 1905 A.D.—
Sant Ji Maharaj remained calm

In 1905 A.D., a very serious earthquake shook the Northern part of India and caused great damage to property and life. Its main centre was Kangra District. It was early morning. As the Kirtan of Asa-Di-Var was going on, the whole Gurdwara was shaken. Sangat rushed out, but Sant Ji remained sitting on the dais in perfect calmness. Bhai Kalyan Singh rushed in the hall and requested Sant Ji to leave the place and come out. But he replied, "Where should I go? Satguru Granth Sahib is here, whom I cannot leave. This is Akal Purkh Himself." He did not leave the place and continued sitting in meditation for a long time, during which the shocks continued but no harm was caused.

Do not be proud of your physique

A Sewadar, named Bhai Sham Singh, used to carry an extraordinary big weight of mud etc., while doing service at the construction work. He was extraordinary strong and was very proud of his well built body. One evening, Sant Ji Maharaj directed him to collect empty baskets. He replied, "An ordinary man can do this work. Kindly ask him." He was asked three times to do this, but he refused, thinking a man of ordinary physique can perform this light duty. Then one lean person collected the empty baskets.

During the night Bhai Sham Singh fell ill. He began suffering from very serious disease and blood started coming out from his intestines. This continued for three days, he suffered great pains and became very weak, thin and lean. On the fourth day he saw Sant Ji and fell at his feet and submitted, "Kindly pardon me." Sant Ji observed, "I have done nothing. I have said nothing to you. This is the result of your own pride and evil conduct. Do service of the Satguru as a humble devotee. Satguru will do good to you."

Order of Sant Ji not to beat the thief

Once at the night, a thief came to commit theft in the Gurdwara Sahib Mastuana. Bhai Sham Singh and others arrested him. He was tied hand and foot with rope and was confined in the back garden. When Sant Ji Maharaj came to know about this, he ordered that none should beat the thief, because he himself and not the thief would feel the effect of beating. So the thief was not beaten. After the Bhog of Asa-Di-Var, Sant Ji came straight to the thief and ordered that he should be released from confinement. Bhai Sham Singh enquired from Sant Ji Maharaj, "Sir, will this thief also get the fruit of the sight of the true Saint ?" Sant Ji Maharaj replied, "Yes." Immediately thief fell at the feet of Sant Ji Maharaj and promised not to commit theft in future and even his family members would not commit theft.

Without Service of the Satguru and the Sangat, Humility cannot be achieved

In order to spread the Religion of the Name and to administer Khande-Da-Amrit, Sant Ji on the request of the devotees used to go to their villages. Once the Sangat of the village 'Dan Singh Wala' took Sant Ji to their village. Bhai Lal Singh Mastuana came to pay respects to Sant Ji, two or three times. Sant Ji said to Bhai Lal Singh, "O Bhai Lal Singh, in the Kingdom of Satguru Nanak, Sewa (service with hands and otherwise) is a very essential duty of a Sikh. You must join in the Sewa (in the construction) of the Gursagar complex and the Sacred Tank. Along with it, practise the meditation on the Name. Without Sewa the I-am-ness of the man does not vanish, although he may devote as much time as he likes in the Religious Meditation etc. Without Sewa, transmigration does not come to an end."

Bhai Lal Singh began sleeping on the ground, near Sant Ji Maharaj at night. All of a sudden Bhai Lal Singh woke up at 2 a.m. one night. He was astonished to see Sant Ji sitting in meditation on the couch. He got up and sat on the ground for meditation. After a few moments, Sant Ji Maharaj noticed him sitting on the ground and observed, "Bhai Ji, as yet, good part of night is still left. You better lie down and take rest. My daily routine of Nit Nem takes a good deal of time and I finish it before 2 a.m. Then I become absorbed in the Shabad (the Word). So I have to get up much before 2 a.m."

Biggest Supernatural Powers etc., which control the World etc., are the results of Repetition of the Name and the Worship

Many persons used to get Supreme joy by meeting Sant Ji. One day, Sant Attar Singh Ji of Atlewala came and stayed at Mastuana. He enjoyed the association of Sant Attar Singh Ji. One day S. Prem Singh of Rajon Majra, who was a minister in the Jind State, came and he was so much attracted towards spiritualism with the Grace of Sant Ji that he became a changed man. After a few days, the foundation of the Gurdwara Sri Guru Singh Sabha, Sangrur, was laid.

In those days a procession in connection with the coronation of the Raja of Sangrur was to take palce. Sant Ji Maharaj was requested to join the procession. A dangerous elephant, which could not be easily controlled was mischieviously sent to Sant Ji. He sat on it. It was miraculous to see that the elephant became wholly innocent, like a lamb, throughout the long period of passing of the procession.

A new power house was being constructed in Sangrur in those days. Sant Attar Singh Ji happened to visit it. The foreman explained to him as to how with the help of magnets etc., the plant worked and the machinery rotated. Sant Ji Maharaj then observed, "If the Name is repeated at all times with sincerity, after keeping the Satguru in mind, an unlimited Powerful Current and Strength results. It is with this power that the universes, worlds, planets, suns and moons are controlled and regulated."

All Charms, Magics etc. become wholly Powerless when the Name is repeated and Gurbani is read

One day, when Sant Ji Maharaj was staying at Mota Majra, Bhai Lal Singh submitted, "Sir, I have heard that charms, magics etc., are very powerful and effective." Sant Ji Maharaj observed, "In the presence of the Gurbani, all these charms etc., and occult powers become wholly powerless and ineffective. It is the duty of the Sikhs to remain absorbed throughout in the Name and Gurbani. Then Sant Ji Maharaj quoted two verses from Gurbani. Translation of these is : "Nama (Bhagat Nam Dev) says, O Tarlochan (Bhagat) ! repeat and keep in your mouth the Name (of the Supreme Being). (Then) go on doing your daily works with your hands and feet, but always keep God (the Lord of Mammon) in your heart." Sant Ji Maharaj then observed, "When God protects the true devotee, no magic etc. or enemy can cause any damage to him."

Controversies and arguments cause grief

Bhai Lal Singh has rendered great service in the orphanage at Gujranwala. Once, he came to Gurusar Sahib, Mastuana on the Maghi fair. He attended the Diwan and delivered a speech. He criticised some beliefs etc. Some Sikhs from the audience, who did not like his ideas, used objectionable language against him. After the Bhog, Sant Ji with affection, consoled him and observed, "It is better that during Kirtan, no topic should be touched. But if some controversy arises, then hear others calmly and think about the matter. Arguments and counter arguments cause grief." Then he advised him that the Satguru himself has ordered that fights or contentions or scuffles result in grief. He further observed that only a rare and True Saint can tolerate and treat alike honour and dishonour. He quoted Gurbani.

Supernatural 'Singhs' keep watch around True Saints

Once, when Sant Ji had stayed near the Jehlum river, strange events were noticed by Bhai Gopal Singh. He talked with Bhai Narain Singh and said, "I saw an amazing scene at night, after the Bhog (close) of the Diwan. A very stoutly built horseman, with a very brilliant face was riding around the tent of Sant Ji. He circumambulated even around other tents. I think he was the Tenth Satguru himself. Let us go and enquire about this from Sant Ji." On the second night, both Bhai Gopal Singh and Bhai Narain Singh sat at some distance from the tent of Sant Ji and they saw that a heavenly horseman circumambulated around the tent of Sant Ji. The most wonderful thing was that the horse trotted of three sides of the earth and also on the fourth side on the surface of the Jehlum river with perfect ease. After each circumambulation, the heavenly horseman would loudly proclaim 'Sat Siri Akal'. Bhai Narain Singh kept quiet; but Bhai Gopal Singh would utter in reply 'Gur-Bar-Akal'. All these events simply amazed them. On the next morning after the Bhog of morning Diwan, they saw Sant Ji and narrated the events, seen by them. Then they enquired what all these events were ? They themselves submitted, "We think that the Tenth Satguru himself came on the horse back." On this, Sant Ji Maharaj observed, "Satguru Gobind Singh is unique. Like him none appeared in this world and none will appear in future. But this is true that his soldiers do come to protect Sikhs like us i.e. (his humble servants)." Sant Ji then warned that "If ever some-one sees such events, he should keep mum and never tell these to anybody."

Thieves and True Saints cannot live at the same place. Concealment of money by Ragis (professional performers of music of Gurbani)

From Jehlum, Sant Ji went to Gujjar Khan. There, as usual, evening and morning Diwans were held. Men, women and children got Khande-Da-Amrit. In those days, the flooring work was going on in Gur Sagar Sahib, Mastuana. Sant Ji then started for the town of Tarakki and came on foot up to Missa Kaswan. Sant Ji directed Bhai Kalyan Singh that offerings made at Gujjar Khan should be spent on purchasing and sending a wagon of stone for the flooring to Mastuana Sahib. On counting, the amount found with them was Rupees 683. The price etc., for the stone, needed was Rupees 700. Sant Ji ordered all the followers to surrender whatever amounts they possessed. All complied with this order. In spite of this, there was a shortage of Rupees 7 only. Ragis kept quiet and did not unfold the covering clothes of their harmoniums. Sant Ji ordered the Jatha to do so and to unscrew the upper part of their harmoniums. On doing so, Rupees 7 were found concealed there. On this Sant Ji ordered these Ragis to leave the place at once. The followers of Sant Ji then humbly requested to pardon them. Then the Ragis also with folded hands begged pardon. Sant Ji now excused them and allowed them to stay with him.

No shortage of food takes place in the homes of Sincere Devotees

After leaving Tarakki, Sant Ji came to the village Bishan Daur, the village of Bhai Hukam Singh at his request. He came with him from Gujjar Khan. When he reached his house he intended that hot food might be served to Sant Ji and his Jatha. Those were winter days. He got cooked pulses and vegetables and also loaves of bread. He invited other Sikh Sangat also. Thirteen members of the Jatha of Sant Ji were also there. The Sangat sat in lines. However, inspite of quick efforts of the women folk, the plates, placed before the Sangat, looked empty. Bhai Hukam Singh felt very nervous and thought that he would face disgrace. He thought of collecting food from the neighbours. Sant Ji at once called Bhai Hukam Singh and ordered him to bring whatever food was in his house. On his lifting the cloth of the basket, he was amazed to find that it was completely filled with hot loaves of bread, which Bhai Hukam Singh served to all. His mother was equally wonder-struck to see this miracle and they fell at the feet of Sant Ji who smiled and observed, "No sincere Sikh of Satguru Nanak can ever face any shortage of anything."

One should not tell others about his elevated Spiritual State

Bhai Mehar Singh was in service in the Military Audit Department. He came in contact with Sant Ji who was pleased to give him necessary Religious Guidance. He went on attending Diwans of Sant Ji. In due course, as a result of his devoted service, he obtained the gift of the Name. He practised the methods, explained to him by Sant Ji for sometime in a sincere way. He noticed very fascinating and joyful condition of his innerself. Although he was instructed not to disclose this to anyone, yet he talked with Bhai Kalyan Singh regarding the same.

Due to this subtle sense of pride, his chain of meditation broke.

Find the Name by reading Sri Guru Granth Sahib

When Sant Ji was going in the train to Bannu, Rai Bahadur Lala Chaman Lal Advocate was also sitting in the same compartment. He was attracted by the spiritualism of Sant Ji. He came near him and paid respect and then requested, "Kindly write a charm for me." Sant Ji observed, "The repetition of the Name 'Waheguru' is the biggest charm and magic. Repeat this." Then he submitted, "Sir, Kindly give me the gift of the Name that is Gur Mantar." Sant Ji replied, "Read Sri Guru Granth Sahib and you will obtain Gur Mantar from the Satguru."

Shahid Singhs performed Kirtan

Sant Ji used to make programmes at the spur of the moment. He was extremely kind-hearted. He was ready to fulfil the wishes of the devotees and to accompany them to propagate, the True Religion of Satguru Nanak Dev Ji Maharaj. His ever-smiling face attracted all towards Spiritualism. One day, after the Evening Diwan, Sant Ji remained sitting calmly. He was silently absorbed in meditation. None had the courage to tell him to move onwards. The Sangat requested Granthi Hari Singh Ji to make request to Sant Ji Maharaj for Kirtan. He obeyed the Sangat and went near Sant Ji and requested, "Sir, will the Kirtan of Asa-Di-Var be performed here ?" Sant Ji replied, "Bhai Ji, we have to perform the Kirtan tomorrow of Baba Ji's Gurbani. We may do this here or elsewhere. It does not make any difference. It is evening time now." Hardly were these words spoken, when the melodious sound of singing Divine Hymns was heard. Bhai Hari Singh thought that some Jatha, singing Shabads, was coming from outside, to pay respects to Sant Ji. Sometime later, Granthi Ji again sought permission to recite the night prayer 'Kirtan Sohila' and said, "May we stay here ?" As soon as Bhai Ji uttered these words, the Shabad Kirtan stopped. The whole Sangat searched for the Jatha who was performing Kirtan; but not a single man could be found. When all efforts to find them failed, the Sangat prayed to Sant Ji, "The Jatha performing Kirtan must have lost the way. We have searched for them but no man has been traced." Sant Ji Maharaj then observed, "You said that Kirtan should be performed here, so God had sent a Jatha for this purpose and the Kirtan was started. But when you talked about reciting Kirtan Sohila, the Kirtan stopped. The Religious Mandates (Maryada) for the Shahid Singhs is very strict. They do not utter even a single word after Kirtan Sohila.

The story of Malik Mohan Singh and his son Malik Hardit Singh I.C.S.

Malik Mohan Singh of Rawalpindi and his wife had great respect for Sant Ji. Their son Malik Hardit Singh had to go to England to pass I.C.S. examination. They invited Sant Ji to their house and submitted, "Sir, be kind to our son. Give your protecting hand to him and confer your blessings on the occasion of his departure to England." Sant Ji Maharaj was pleased to give to the youngman a Gutka of Nit Nem (book containing Daily Sikh Prayers) and advised him, "O youngman, never miss the daily prayers. Satguru Nanak Dev Ji will be ever with you." Malik Hardit Singh I.C.S., subsequently became an Ambassador.

The Divine Hymns contain Divine Sermons

Once Sant Ji came to Rawalpindi at the invitation of Malik Mohan Singh and stayed in his house. Sant Ji asked all his family members to recite one Shabad each. When the turn of Malik Hardit Singh came, who was at that time 12 years of age, he recited one Divine Hymn of the Ninth Satguru.

After hearing this, Sant Ji Maharaj observed, "You have recited this Shabad with a view to give to me this Sermon." On hearing these words, showing utmost humility of mind, all were pleased and amazed to note such a great height of Spiritual Status and most saintly character of Sant Ji.

This body is foreign

Once, Sant Ji was wearing a sheet of foreign cloth. when he came to Rawalpindi. At that time agitation against use of foreign cloth and other things was at its height. However, Sant Ji being a perfect Brahmgiani was indifferent to such ideas. A young congressman in a most obstinate and foolish manner used improper words and after pulling one side of his sheet said, "Do you not know that this sheet is made of foreign cloth ?" Sant Ji replied, "O dear boy, even my body is foreign." This is a solid truth, which only a Brahmgiani ever remembers and realises.

Four hundred and fifty shots fired on the aeroplane, yet it returned back safe

During the first world war (1914 to 1918 A.D.) Malik Hardit Singh served in the Air Force, as a pilot. During an attack of the Germans, his aeroplane flew in their midst. The enemy planes showered bullets on the plane of Malik Hardit Singh and tried to smash it. Although it was badly damaged, yet he succeeded in bringing it back to its base. This was naturally due to the Divine Protection. It was a miracle to see that although the plane had 450 marks of gunshots and two bullet injuries were caused on the body of Malik Hardit Singh, yet he came back safe. As soon as he came to India, he went straight to Sant Ji to pay his respects. He bowed before him. Sant Ji enquired, "Malik Hardit Singh, how did you fare in the war ?" Malik Hardit Singh had hardly opened his lips to tell the story of the plane, when Sant Ji observed, "All this is known to me. You please tell something else." Malik Hardit Singh's belief that it was due to the Grace of Sant Ji that he was saved, bacame most strong. Tears were flowing from his eyes and his voice was chocked due to emotions. Those present also felt similar sensation and were amazed to know all this. Their esteem and respect for Sant Ji Maharaj was greatly enhanced.

Visit to Bara Mula (Kashmir)—Crossing of River Jehlum inspite of Strong Storm

Sant Ji went to Kashmir. He stayed in a houseboat at Bara Mula for some time. One day, Sant Singh of Dhamli requested Sant Ji to oblige him by eating meals (Langar) at his house, which was on the other side of the river. When the Sangat and Sant Ji were ready to start, a very strong storm began blowing. The boatmen refused to take their boats on the other side. They submitted that the boats would sink in view of the storm. Sant Ji consoled them and asked them to sing a particular Divine Hymn. Then he directed the boatmen to ply their boats. All went to the other side safe and sound.

CHAPTER X

VISIT TO SRINAGAR—MEETING WITH BHAI KAHAN SINGH OF NABHA— VISITED PATIALA AND DELHI DARBAR

From Bara Mula, Sant Ji went to Sri Nagar, Bhai Kahan Singh of Nabha came to pay respects to him. He paid respects to Sant Ji. He was glad to note that the Divine Hymns sung by Sant Ji Maharaj in his most melodious voice had most extraordinary and magical effect on the minds of all. Bhai Kahan Singh found that Sant Ji was a Brahmgiani, the Knower of the Secrets of human beings and Super Soul, well-wisher and helper of all, and most calm and humble. Such most gifted souls come in this world very seldom to save all the humanity. Bhai Sahib heard Sant Ji's Shabad sung in different musical measures also.

Visit to Patiala on the Invitation of Maharaja Bhupinder Singh and other events

Maharaja Bhupinder Singh after becoming Maharaja, showed a great interest in Gurmat (Sikh Religion and its propagation). He ordered that in all courts and offices Gurmukhi should be used. He got his marriage performed strictly in accordance with the rules of Anand Marriage. Then he invited Sant Ji to Patiala to obtain the benefit of Satsang and his blessings. Sant Ji went there and was received with honours. All that happened there was told by Sant Ji Maharaj himself to Bhai (subsequently) Sant Teja Singh Ji. Its translation is given below :

At that time, in the mind of Maharaja there was great love for Satsang and Gurbani. Sant Ji wanted that by staying with him, at least for six months, this love should be made perfect and unshakable. But as ordained by God, he had to leave Patiala due to the conspiracy of some envious persons. From Patiala Sant Ji came to Chakwal to lay the foundation of Chakwal School. After the foundation of the Chakwal School was laid by Sant Ji, he stayed there for some time. Religious Parchar (Sermons on the Sikh Religion) and the administration of Khande-Da-Amrit, as usual, were held on a very large scale. Then he came back to Mastuana Sahib.

Delhi Darbar

In those days, in 1911, preparations were being made on a very large scale for holding a big Darbar on the occasion of the visit of the Emperor George, the Fifth, at Delhi. The Khalsa College Committee passed a resolution, requesting Sant Ji to accompany them as their representative on this occasion and to give the message of the Nectarean Gurbani to all. However, Sant Ji accepted the request of the Jind Darbar which submitted that all necessary arrangements for the stay etc., of Sant Ji at Delhi would be made by that State. Sant Ji accepted this request and sent necessary information regarding this to the Khalsa College Committee, Amritsar.

Sant Ji Maharaj joined the Procession

A big procession started. The second elephant, behind the elephant on which Sri Guru Granth Sahib was placed, was that of Sant Ji. Then followed the elephants, on which other Saints, other Maharajas and Rajas were seated. Then there were the elephants, on which Ragi Jathas were seated. The procession reached Gurdwara

Sahib Sis Ganj. Then it started from Gurdwara Sahib to the Red Fort. The procession finally entered the fort. Here, all the Maharajas, Rajas, Nawabs and Dignitories were sitting in their respective seats. Emperor George the Fifth and the Viceroy held their special seats. A prominent seat was provided for Sant Ji. All were amazed to see the Glowing Face and Heavenly Personality of Sant Ji. The Emperor, pointing towards Sant Ji, asked the Viceroy as to who that magnanimous personality was. He told him that, "He is the Lord Bishop and the Supreme Saint of the Khalsa." Similar answer was given to the Emperor by Maharaja Hira Singh, who said, "He is the Chief Religious Head of the Sikhs. We all enjoy his protection. One Bishop continued looking towards the most Bright Face of Sant Ji Maharaj. He observed, "I have not seen such a holy personality in my life. His august form shows that he owns special Heavenly Powers."

CHAPTER XI

VISIT TO BENARAS AND OTHER EVENTS LAYING THE FOUNDATIONS OF THE HINDU UNIVERSITY BENARAS

In the winter of 1914 A.D., Pandit Madan Mohan Malviya, who was at that time the Secretary of the Hindu University, with utmost respect, requested Sant Ji to grace the occasion of the laying of the foundation of the University. He requested Sant Ji to perform five Akhand

Paths of Sri Guru Granth Sahib, who accepted this request. In one of the most beautiful camps in the vast grounds of the University, Sant Ji was accommodated. Five Akhand Paths were held there. At the time of the Bhog ceremony, Maharajas and Rajas and other dignitories came to get the Grace of Sant Ji. This was the place where the foundation of the Sanskrit College was to be laid. Melodious Kirtan was performed by Sant Ji.

After the Bhog ceremony, Maharaja Ganga Singh of Bikaner filled a silver basin with cement and mortar. Maharaja Prabhu Narain of Kanshi Raj, offered eleven bricks of gold. Sant Ji filled the foundation of the Sanskrit College with a big gold spoon and put mortar and cement in it. He also put the eleven gold bricks in the foundation, with his hands. He then sang Divine Verses.

Maharaja of Kanshi (Ram Nagar) honoured Sant Ji Maharaj by keeping Him for about one week

After the foundation laying function had finished, Sant Ji was invited by Maharaja Kanshi (Ram Nagar) and on his request Sant Ji stayed there for about one week. Maharaja Sahib requested Sant Ji Maharaj to sit on the throne on which he never sat. It was reserved for Shri Vishav Nath. The Maharaja performed all rites and ceremonies when he seated Sant Ji on that throne.

Two Sadhus became Singhs

At that time, two students were getting Religious Instructions in the Niranjani Akhara, Asi Ghat, Bhadaini. They attended the functions at the Hindu University. They were changed by seeing the high personality of Sant Ji Maharaj. They intended to invite him and to serve meals to him. On the appointed day, they took Sant Ji for that purpose at their place. When they all sat in line for taking meals, Sant Ji Maharaj said to Pandit Ilaichi Ram and his companion, "Brethern you are Sadhus, then why do you get your long hair cut. Until you make a promise that you will not do so in future, I will not take meals." On this, Pandit Ilaichi Ram said, "Sir, if I keep long hair my eyes become red and sore." The other Sadhu submitted, "Sir, if I keep long hair, pain starts in my teeth." Sant Ji Maharaj asked both of them to sit in his front. Then he sprinkled water on the eyes of one and on the teeth of the other. He said, "Brethern keep long hair and none of you will ever get the trouble, that you complained of." The lucky Sadhus obeyed the words of Sant Ji Maharaj. They kept long hair and took Khande-Da-Amrit. They never got that trouble after that.

Sikh Educational Conferences—Sant Ji conferred his Grace on these occasions

Sant Ji used to attend almost all the Sikh Educational Conferences. These were important gatherings, where Panthic programmes were conducted and chalked out. The Religious Diwans, on these occasions had great influence on the Sangat. Sant Ji took major part in these. Lacs of devotees got true colour of the Name and became Singhs by taking Khande-Da-Amrit.

Advancement of Sikhs will take concrete shape only when all get up at 3 a.m. and perform worship as ordered by the Satgurus

Sant Ji used to observe, "All have got great desire that the Sikhs should make advancement in all directions. But please do remember and firmly believe that this can be possible only when in the first place, each day, early morning at 3 a.m, you all get up from your beds and sounds of taking baths on the wells etc., of the village and cities are heard and then melodious sounds of 'Sat Naam' are heard on all sides. In the second place, when you all contribute one tenth of your income and contribute whatever else you want to give in the common treasure of the Khalsa Panth, every month or every year, then no appeal need be made for Panthic projects and Institutions. By making appeals, the mind become weak and timid. Although in compliance with the wishes of the Sangat, I had to make an appeal for funds at the Fourth Conference, held at Gujranwala, yet my internal voice is that this is not proper. It is a different matter if some responsible persons sit under the protection of the Nishan Sahib and the devotees voluntarily pay whatever amounts they want to pay. The necessary prayer for conferment of the Name can be then made at the spot. Thirdly all the wings of the Panth and all Sikhs should repeat and remember the Name and perform Hari Kirtan and must do all business in Gurmukhi letters."

To attach one's mind constantly with the Name just as the clock goes on striking 'tick, tick' is the only best job to be done by the mortal

Sant Ji used to observe, "The primary Religious duty of every man is to repeat the Name just as the clock goes on striking 'tick, tick'. Every Sikh should attach his mind with each breath with the Name." Again, again, and again remember God. Drink this Nectar (of the Naam) and satiate the thirst of the mind and the body. Please take care of every breath. Do not allow any breath to go waste."

Equal treatment for all the Sangat is essential

One day, when Bhog was to be performed, out of respect for Sant Ji, a blanket was spread on the *duree*, where he had to sit. He slowly removed the blanket and sat on the *duree* where other Sikhs were sitting.

He observed, "All persons come as human beings after transmigration. They have got a right to obtain the Divine Knowledge (Gian). Some obtain this soon and others get it after many births." Sant Ji explained this thus :

"There are two ladies. Both have to lit fire in the fire-place in the morning for cooking food. One is wise enough to put in it first thin straws, then some thin pieces of dried wood and then some big pieces of wood, for use in the morning. The other is a foolish woman. She fills the fire-place in the morning with thick wood pieces and wet dung-cakes etc. The former lits one match-stick and the fire is lit in a very short time. The other one has to lit many match-sticks and blow many times the firewood, yet it does not burn. It takes a very long time to burn the same. In the same way, those seekers of the Truth, who strictly obey the mandates of the Gurbani and are regular in making attempts to control their minds get Gian (Divine Knowledge) with one Glance of the True Guru, while others, who do not observe these mandates, have to wait for years to obtain the Name after great difficulties."

Appeal for Funds should not be made in the Diwan

Sant Ji used to observe, "When appeal for funds is made in the conference, many persons start leaving their seats. This creates great unpleasantness. When some Sikhs donate one or two rupee or small sums, nobody cares for them, but when somebody gives five hundred or one thousand rupees, long prayers are made for him. In this way, the feelings of differentiation take birth. This is also another form of mammon. 'Sat Sri Akal' is also then uttered loudly. The old system was that the man, who had to perform prayers used to sit in separate place, Donations were made there. Whether amount offered was a pice or one lac, similar prayers were offered for all. He used to say 'Please Utter Waheguru'. The Sikh offers donation, may he remember the Name. The Sikh Sangat (audience) would then calmly sit on their seats and hear Kirtan with devotion. Resolution could be passed without disturbance. None will try to go away then. Sadh Sangat is the Supreme Power. It can change the system. Make your minds strong."

Brahmgiani remains merged in the Name

Sant Ji used to observe, "I am the citizen of that country, where castes, sub-castes and dynasty do not exist. There people do not meet each other in bodily forms. They meet through the 'Shabad' (the Name). They, having become part of the Shabad, the Supreme Being can be met by those, who themselves gain that status."

Arya Samaj family took Amrit

One day, when Sant Ji Maharaj had made preparation to leave Hyderabad, an old lady submitted, "Sir, I have come to know that you are now leaving us. Kindly come to my house and take meals there. My son has gone out. If he is lucky, he will come and have your Sight." Some devotees, who were sitting there submitted, "Sir, this lady is full of devotion, but her family members are

Arya Samajis and talk ill of the Satguru, therefore, it is not proper to go to their house and do not take food there." Sant Ji observed, "Sadh Sangat Ji, if I do not visit their house and I do not tell them about the Sikh Religion, then how will they come under the protection of Satguru Nanak Dev Ji. This opportunity is created by God for their reformation." Sant Ji agreed to take meals in the house of the old lady. On the next day, she prepared food for Sant Ji with great devotion. He went there alongwith Sangat. It so happened that the son of the old lady also came there, before taking meals. The Nectarean Sermons delivered by Sant Ji Maharaj had magical effect on her son. He was a changed man now. He fell at the feet of Sant Ji Maharaj, and submitted, "Sir, my past life has gone waste. I have been deprived of the true love of Satguru Nanak Dev Ji. I am now extremely sorry for my mistakes. Kindly shower your Grace on us and fill us with love for Satguru Sahib." Sant Ji Maharaj heard his whole story and infused in the whole family such love for Truth that they were now full of devotion and love for the Satguru and Sikh Religion. They left smoking.

CHAPTER XII

THE SHABAD IS THE TRUE GURU—
OTHER SERMONS—MORE EVENTS

Sant Ji used to explain, "Satguru Nanak Dev Ji observes, 'The Shabad (the Name) is the True Guru and the attachment of mind with it is the disciple.'" Sant Ji explained that Deh-Dhari Guru never existed. Before Satguru Nanak Dev Ji left this world and merged in the Supreme Being, he was no doubt seen in the physical body; but he, in fact, existed and will ever exist in the form of Ever-living Shabad. He has proclaimed that Shabad is True Guru and attachment of mind with it is the disciple."

Sant Ji Maharaj then said, "There is absolutely no spiritual gain by becoming a Deh-Dhari Guru. He, who has realised the Supreme Soul or the True Immortal God, leaves all kinds of pride and I-am-ness."

"By abandoning ego, the True Status of the True Sikh is obtained. Where there is artificiality, there is the ego and the I-am-ness of the physical body never ends. How can such a person, who has not succeeded in wiping off his own ego, enable others to abandon it ?"

Panth Defined

Sant Ji once observed, "Panth means Path. Panth does not mean a majority. Panth consists of those Sikhs, who travel on the Path shown by the Satguru Kalgidhar Maharaj." Then he quoted these words of the Satguru, "He who lives according to my prescribed Laws, is my Sikh. Such one is my master and I am his servant."

Mata Ji (Respected Mother of Sant Ji Maharaj) merged in the Supreme Being

Mata Ji (Respected Mother of Sant Ji) was lying ill in her room at Gur Sagar Sahib Mastuana. There was no hope of her survival. Sant Ji was aware of this. When the Sangat told him about her condition, he observed, "There is no danger to Mata Ji. She will live for two years more.

This will relieve her of coming one new birth after her death, that is, after this suffering for two years, her transmigration will end and she will merge in the Creator."

Now the time of her merger with the Supreme Being will come after she remains ill for two years more. Inspite of the fact that she had become extremely weak and could not take any solid food, her face was Bright and she remained busy in repeating the Name 'Waheguru' till her last breath. She expired and reached the Home of the Satguru. The entire atmosphere resounded with Name. Sant Ji was performing Kirtan. After the Bhog, he came to the quarter of Mata Ji. All necessary ceremonies for carrying the body on the bier had already been completed. The bier was lifted by the devotees. Thousands of the Sikhs were walking slowly in front and also at the back of the bier. They were all singing Divine Hymns. Sant Ji followed the bier. Sant Ji observed that the worship performed by Mata Ji in many human births, has borne Divine Fruit (freedom from transmigration) now.

After some time, the procession reached Akal Bunga. The burning pyre was ready near it. The dead body of Mata Ji was placed on it, with due respects. Then fire was given to the pyre. After the performance of Kirtan of Divine Hymns and recitation of Kirtan Sohila, Ardas was performed. The Sangat went back to attend the Diwan. The singing of the Divine Hymns for two days and night continued. On the third day Sant Ji Maharaj said, "Do not search the burnt pyre. The ashes and all else should be buried in the earth." This direction was followed.

How Universal Peace will prevail in the World ?

Sant Ji used to observe regarding Mastuana as follows :

"Please see that the Mastuana Sahib flourished by leaps and bounds. An Educational Centre is to be established here, Universal love is to be infused in the students, so that the condition prevalent in Satyug (the age of Truth) may be again revived. In that age, the True Rishis and Sants spread universal brotherhood and worship of Supreme Being everywhere, and no false ways, customs or practices existed."

Regarding True Peace and Real Freedom in India, he used to observe, "This will happen, when throughout the villages and cities, all will earn their livelihood by fair and honest means and when they will maintain one common kitchen by. contributing their income in it and when they will perform marriages and other social programmes through the same common kitchen.

CHAPTER XIII

THE SEWA (CONSTRUCTION WORK) AT DAMDAMA SAHIB AND MORE TOPICS

Satguru Kalgidhar Ji Maharaj had prophecied that "the Sewa of Damdama Sahib would be undertaken by Attar Singh." When Sant Ji Maharaj went to Guru Ki Kanshi, Damdama Sahib, there was an extraordinary huge gathering in the Diwan, held at the Kacha Platform, where the Satguru used to hold Diwans, Sant Ji saw that there was only a Kacha Tank. He prayed to the Satguru and felt very much that no steps were taken uptil then to construct all these works in bricks, marble, mortar etc. He impressed upon the audience the urgent need of undertaking these works. He appealed to them thus, "O dear Sadh Sangat, the Words, uttered by Sri Satguru Teg Bahadur Sahib were not fulfilled uptil now. Let us all now serve the great cause, through our bodies, hands and wealth and let us make the sacred tank Pucca." As soon as the appeal was made, many thousand rupees were donated by the Sangat. Then Sant Ji visited the cottage of the Behangams (permanent devotees and honorary servants of Satguru) and said to them, "Please give whatever money you possess. He, who conceals, that will take birth as a donkey." The fortunate ones parted with their amounts. Seventeen thousands rupees were thus collected. The entire amount was handed over to the Managing Committee of Damdama Sahib, constituted by the Khalsa High School and they were told to make the Sacred Tank Pucca.

During his stay at Kanjala, Sant Ji Maharaj used to tell the visitors to make contributions for the Sewa at Damdama Sahib, in money or in kind

One day at Kanjla, Sant Ji Maharaj addressed the Sangat and observed, "Brethern, in the house of Satguru Nanak Dev Ji, all powers are present. By his kindness, a canal of gold can be built from this place upto Damdama Sahib, but the Satguru does not want this to be done, as he has to give to you chances to make your bodies, mind and wealth fruitful. Do not feel shy of making contributions. Please do this according to your capacities and do sacrifice all for the Tenth Satguru. The Satguru has not kept secret or concealed anything from you. He says, that his mind, body, wealth belongs to my Sikhs."

Maharaja Bhupinder Singh offered to bear all expenses of construction at Damdama Sahib, but Sant Ji politely refused this and said, "This is to be done by all and you can also make contributions. I want that everybody should obtain the fruits of Sewa. You can also, according to your capacity, take part in it and obtain the blessings of the Satguru, the True King."

Sant Ji Maharaj personally visited in a rickshaw, several persons also at Shimla to get contributions

Sant Ji Maharaj had such a great desire to complete the Sewa at Guru Ki Kanshi, Damdama Sahib, that for the first time in his whole life, he went to collect donations at Shimla. When he used to meet donors, he would say, "Brethren, a beggar, like me, will never meet you again." Others who used to come and see him, were also persuaded, to make contributions, according to their capacities."

When God is Kind, no shortage of any kind will be experienced—Miracles at Shimla

One day, at Shimla, Sardar Sunder Singh Chhabra requested Sant Ji Maharaj to take meals at his house in his quarter in Nabha-house. After the Bhog of the Diwan, in the Gurdwara, Sant Ji Maharaj declared, "No one should go without taking food at the Langar." There were more than one thousand devotees. Sardar Sunder Singh Chhabra had made arrangements for food for about two hundred persons. When the ladies of the house came to know that the entire Sangat would take food, they became nervous and could not think as to what should be done then. On seeing their worried condition, Sant Ji Maharaj observed, "Daughters, do not be nervous. Cover the Langar with a sheet and go on serving food for all. Continue throughout reciting these two verses from Gurbani.

This order of Sant Ji Maharaj was obeyed. After serving food to all, a lot of it remained unconsumed.

Sach Khand described—The state of attachment of mind and heart with the Supreme Being in His Formless Form after discarding three modes of mammon results in reaching Sach Khand

Professor Ganga Singh, the renowned Sikh preacher used to perform the Katha (i.e. explain the messages and implications of Gurbani), in those days, at the Gurdwara Singh Sabha at Shimla, after Sant Ji used to finish the Kirtan of Asa-Di-Var each day. One day, the professor explained the meanings of the words 'Sach Khand' after quoting some parts of Gurbani. One day, when he went to pay respects to Sant Ji at the place where Sant Ji was staying, he asked the Professor, "The other day you drew a nice description of Sach Khand. If you have seen it, please show this to me also." The Professor with folded hands, submitted, "Maharaj, I have given description of Sach Khand on the basis of my book knowledge. I have not seen it. You have seen it. Kindly show this to me also." On hearing this, Sant Ji sat in deep meditation. The Divine Glow came on his face. The whole atmosphere was filled with it. Professor Ganga Singh himself says, "The Supreme Joy that I got on that day, has never been felt by me in my whole life. The Divine and Nectarean feelings entered even my each hair. However, I cannot describe this in words."

There will be no Transmigration of the Soul of a Devotee who sacrifices all for the Satguru

The main founders of the Satsang at Shimla was Bhai Amar Singh. He was also called Sant Amar Singh. He came to pay respects to Sant Ji. Sant Ji said to him, "You also please make contribution as Sewa for the Gurdwara at Damdama Sahib and then obtain the blessings of Satguru Kalgidhar Ji Maharaj." Bhai Amar Singh with folded hands submitted, "True King, I shall let you know about this tomorrow." The next day, after office work he went to his house and then came back and saw Sant Ji. His savings of the whole life were placed before Sant Ji. On seeing such a great faith of this devoted Sikh, Sant Ji observed, "On surrendering body, mind and wealth before the Satguru, the devotee gets this Grace by obeying his Command." Then Sant Ji said, "O brother Sikh, you are blessed one. You will not have to again take births (i.e your transmigration will finish)."

The Tenth Door—Meanings explained

One day Bhai Shanker Singh enquired from Sant Ji Maharaj at Nabha House, Shimla, as to what was meant by 'Tenth Door'. Sant Ji observed, "Leave the three modes of mammon i.e., Rajo, Tammo and Sato i.e., (i) the mode of the mind when it acts as that of a rich man and gives charity etc., (2) the mode when he commits sins and evils and then (3) the mode in which he performs virtues under the influence of egoism. When the seeker leaves these three modes, he enters the Fourth State of mind i.e., he ever remains attached with the Formless Supreme Being and he enters the Tenth Door." Sant Ji Maharaj quoted a verse which means, "By repeating and remembering the Name, Divine Knowledge and Light which is much more brilliant than even crores of suns, is gained. Then the darkness of duality vanishes."

Ardas (Final Prayer) should not be long—The method of doing so explained

Whenever Sant Ji used to go for Amrit Parchar and propagating the Sikh Religion, there used to be crowds on very large scales. One day, Sant Ji Maharaj recited the evening prayer (Rehras), (as directed by Bhai Mani Singh Sahib and Baba Deep Singh Sahib). He himself performed the final Ardas. After this he declared, "Ardas should not be very long. At the time of Ardas, all the Ten Satgurus attend it, standing on their 'angutha' (first toe). After reciting the names of the Satgurus and the Martyrs, a short and humble request specifying the purpose for which Ardas is read should be made."

Abide by God's Will—Do not speak harsh words—Ignore minor matters—Take Amrit

On certain occasions, when objections were raised by some proud scholars etc., Sant Ji would observe : "God has ordained us not to talk ill of anyone. Whatever He does is proper. Abide by His Will. This is the best course. Minor objections regarding the way to reach Satguru are not proper.

"If both husband and wife do not come together for taking Amrit, then give Amrit to even one of them, the person incharge of the ship, has to give ticket to anyone (whether a man or a woman) who comes to the person concerned. They may take this ticket even together. Sometimes the couple do not come together. How can

97

I refuse the ticket to anyone, who wants to enter the Kingdom of the Tenth Satguru. We administer Amrit, after fully impressing upon them the need to observe all the mandates which are fully explained beforehand. One, who disobeys will suffer the consequences."

Sant Ji used to explain as to who is a True Khalsa in this way, "Please do remember that to become a True Khalsa, one has to travel a most difficult path. Until the internal Divine Light is seen, no one can claim himself to be a True Khalsa. We never think of that and never search for that which we must do. We stress minor matters and objections. These cause hindrance in our True Path and do not allow us to proceed further towards the Divine Goal."

Sweepers etc. should also be given Amrit and treated as brethren

One day, an old Sikh asked Sant Ji Maharaj, "The Singh Sabha administers Khande-Da-Amrit, even to sweepers and shoe-makers. I have doubt about this. Kindly enlighten us whether this should be done or not or whether it is proper." Sant Ji recited relevent parts, touching this matter from the Gurbani and from the Divine Hymns of the Tenth Satguru and asserted, "There is no such thing as castes or creeds. The Gurus had no belief in these, nor do I believe these. The Satguru have declared that the caste of all human beings is the same."

How to become a saint explained

One day, Professor Harbans Singh submitted before Sant Ji Maharaj, "How can we become like you ?" Sant Ji Maharaj observed, "All of you are like me. The features, the parts of the body etc., of you are like me." The

Professor again submitted, "Kindly tell us how we can attain Spiritual Status like you ?" Sant Ji Maharaj replied, "Please get up early morning and take bath. Then recite Gurbani." He again said, "If we still feel sleepy, then what should be done ?" Sant Ji Maharaj replied, "Wash your face with water, again." He again enquired, "Maharaj, if again the feeling of sleep continues, then what should be done ?" Sant Ji Maharaj observed, "Read Gurbani as loudly as you can." Then the Professor said, "What will be the result of this ?" Sant Ji Maharaj replied, "Do all this and then you will yourself come to know the results."

The Sewa performed by the Ninth and Tenth Satgurus at Damdama Sahib narrated

Sant Ji Maharaj, one day, observed that the Ninth Satguru used to take out mud from the Sacred Guru Sar Tank by gathering the same in his shawl for five times and the Tenth Satguru used to take out the mud in his shield for five times.

The Sewa (free service) maintains physical and mental health and finally takes the Devotee to the Kingdom of the Satguru

The Superintendent of the Khalsa School was also the teacher of Religious lessons, working in the Khalsa High School, Damdama Sahib. He used to bring about forty students with him to perform Sewa at the sacred Guru Sar Tank. They used to ply spades and fill baskets with mud and throw it out, each day. After two or three days, only five students used to come and the remaining used to go to play football and hockey. On enquiry by

Sant Ji asked as to why the number of the students had decreased, the teacher narrated the above reason. On this, Sant Ji observed, "This game of performing Sewa is very difficult, but this game yields many fruits here, as well as in the next world. This gives great strength to the mind as well as the body here and yields Divine Fruits and Liberation also. Do this here, otherwise you will have to repent."

In the face of anger of a naked Sadhu, Sant Ji remained perfectly calm

On the Baisakhi Day, one naked Sadhu performing painful penances, took burning piece of wood and placed it on his shoulder, on seeing Sant Ji. Then he began uttering harsh words against him. After he exhausted himself, Sant Ji Maharaj proceeded further without uttering a single word. He remained perfectly calm and observed, "This saint wanted 'fire' (i.e., use of angry and foul words) from me. However, I have no fire (i.e., I always remain calm and polite)."

Sant Ji Maharaj did not like Special Seat for himself

On the day of the advent of Sri Satguru Gobind Singh Ji Maharaj, Akhand Path was arranged by the Singh Sabha. Sant Ji Maharaj had to perform Kirtan of Asa-Di-Var. A Singh spread a cushion under the seat where Sant Ji Maharaj had to sit. Before taking his seat, he got this cushion removed and observed, "I am not separate from the Sangat. I must sit as the Sangat are sitting. I do not want any special seat for me."

The reason for wearing a sheet of cloth explained by Sant Ji Maharaj—"This indicates a shroud for me."

One day, Sant Ji Maharaj observed, "Sadh Sangat Ji, the sheet of cloth, that I wear, serve the purpose of a turban, a shirt, a pillow, a coat, a waistcoat and quilt also. It serves the purpose of a shroud, which I wear, as I treat myself as a dead man and I have no attachment with the world. Anyone who wants to wear a sheet of cloth like me has to abandon love for mammon, pride and worldly love."

One and a quarter maund of ghee (purified butter) surely supplied in Guru Ka Langar (Free Kitchen) everyday

One day a Sikh came to Damdama Sahib. He brought a cart-load of Bajra (millet) for the free kitchen. Sant Ji directed him to eat food from the Langar. He replied, "Maharaj, I shall eat food at my house. Here only course, dried and stiff loaves are served." Sant Ji thought this man was talking ill of the Guru Ka Langar. He called him and sent for two loaves of bread from the Langar. He directed him to open his palm and then pressed the loaves. Lo ! Ghee (clarified butter) began flowing from the same. He was warned not to talk ill of the Guru Ka Langar. Sant Ji Maharaj then observed, "One and a quarter maund of ghee is secretly supplied by the Supernatural Power in the Langar, everyday.

Ever remember that we have to die—Ever repeat Naam

On the day, the respected mother of Sant Ji Maharaj left this world. Sardar Nihal Singh told Sant Ji Maharaj that his respected mother was very fortunate, because for four days, after this event, continuous Kirtan of Gurbani was performed. On this, Sant Ji Maharaj observed, "You must remember that one day you have to die. All of us will die and so perform as much meditation and reading of Gurbani etc., as is possible."

The worldly riches etc. will remain here. Do not remain attached with these

Bhai Ram Singh submitted at Damdama Sahib, "Maharaj, the officials of the Nabha State want to take possession of the houses, lands etc., of Mastuana." Sant Ji Maharaj observed, "Mastuana does not exist at all. When in a twinkling of an eye all the regions, spheres and worlds are liable to vanish, when doomsday comes, then what is the existence and life of Mastuana." Master Ram Singh then said, "Maharaj, this property is of the Panth and the Sewa is also of the Panth." Sant Ji then observed, "If this is the Sewa of the Panth, then go and do this yourself." He then explained that due to his being employed as a teacher, he was forced not to do so. Sant Ji Maharaj then narrated a story and said, "Somebody caught hold of a pillar and clung to it. He began crying for help saying that the pillar had caught hold of him and was not liberating it. A wise man came there and pulled his arms away from the pillar and said, that you have yourself clasped the pillar. There is no fault of the pillar." Sant Ji Maharaj then said to Master Ram Singh, "Please leave service and come to Mastuana." This had a magical effect on him. He left the service and went to Mastuana to serve there.

CHAPTER XIV

SOME MORE SERMONS AND OTHER MATTERS NARRATED — RELIGIOUS DEEDS DEFINED—GOING TO JAILS NOT A RELIGIOUS DEED

Sant Ji, one day, explained as to what were religious works or deeds. He observed, "To suffer imprisonment in jails in connection with some Panthic or political movement is a religious act. A religious act is that act, by which the seeker travels on the Divine Path to obtain Liberation from the Transmigration, such as performing Kirtan, reciting Gurbani and meditation on the Name and on the Satguru and God."

Congregational Prayers, sincerely made, produce Miracles—Heavy rainfall at Jaito

When Sant Ji Maharaj went to attend the big Diwans at Jaito, it was extremely hot. Thousands of devotees came to attend these. There was great scarcity of water. There were no rains in that particular period. Even drinking water was not easily available. All made requests to Sant Ji to pray for rainfall. Sant Ji quoted a verse from Gurbani that God Himself exists and resides in the Sangat (sincere devotees). Then he observed, "Let us all make prayer. God will certainly accept it." Then Ardas was performed by all standing. Then Sangat took their seats. Then Sant Ji Maharaj in a very loud and melodious voice sang a Divine Hymn, beginning like this :

"Kindly be merciful and send heavy rains." All the Sangat sang the same verse, repeating after Sant Ji sang it. The whole Divine Hymn was sung in this way, by

Sant Ji, followed by the Sangat. Lo! thick clouds gathered in the sky as the prayer was heard and granted by the Supreme Being. Very heavy rains began to fall. This continued for a long time. There was water everywhere. All tanks etc., were now full of water.

Never stand with a Sword (naked or shielded) in front of Sri Guru Granth Sahib, while performing Ardas

One day, when the long prayer was going to be made and all stood up for this purpose before Sri Guru Granth Sahib, an Akali Singh tried to take out his sword from its sheath, with a view to stand with the naked sword in his hands, in front of Guru Granth Sahib. Sant Ji observed, "Please remember that we have to stand with folded hands now and we should not exhibit the sword, while making prayers. Doing so means that we are showing disrespect to the Satguru, who is the Lord of this world and the next one." However, the Akali Singh did not obey this and wanted to draw out his sword from the sheath. But inspite of his best efforts, the sword could not be pulled out. This was a great miracle.

Love of the Satguru for His Sikhs, explained—If the Sikh catches hold of the finger of the True Guru, the latter carries the former in his lap; but if the Sikh does not do so, then he has to weep on account of his obstinacy

When Sant Ji Maharaj was at Sialkot, Bhai Narain Singh enquired from him, "Maharaj, to what extent and in what manner the True Guru helps his Sikhs ?" Sant Ji replied, "I shall make this clear by an illustration. In past days, ladies used to bring water from wells. They used to place one pitcher over the other on their heads. Some used to carry their children also. When the child would weep, the mother would try to pacify the child, but if the child continued to weep obstinately, the mother would leave him or her on the ground. The mother's affection was there, as she was to take the child with her on her way back from the well. If, on return, the child behaved well and held the finger of the mother, she would lift the child and take him or her in her lap, but if the child still wept and would not hold the hand of the mother, she would mildly kick the child saying affectionately 'go on weeping'. In the same way the Satguru helps the Sikh, who holds his finger, and he then carries the Sikh in his lap. However, if the Sikh obstinately ignores the Satguru, then he will have to go on weeping." Sant Ji Maharaj recited some verses touching the subject.

The conduct and duties of a Sikh explained—These are the worship of the Name, God and the Satguru, detachment from mammon, adoption of Divine Knowledge, control of mind and suppression of the Evil instincts

Bhai Narain Singh put another question to Sant Ji Maharaj and enquired as to what should be the duties, conduct etc., of the Sikh ? Sant Ji Maharaj observed, "It is mandatory for a True Sikh of the Satguru observe these commands :

(i) He must meditate upon the Word, the Satguru and one God.

(ii) He must remain detached from mammon.

(iii) He must obtain pure Divine Knowledge.

(iv) His mind must be free from all sinful and evil thoughts and instincts."

Do not write or engrave Gurmukhi Words on the floors

At Sialkot, Sant Ji gave Khande-Da-Amrit to a very large number of persons. Whenever he visited Gurdwara Sahib Babe-Di-Ber, at Sialkot, he was pained to find that names of the donors etc., were written or engraved in Gurmukhi on the floors of the Gurdwara Sahib. He walked very cautiously to avoid putting his feet on these words. He observed, "These words are the hair of Satguru Nanak Dev Ji. It is a sin to write Gurmukhi on the floors."

The story of bravery of Prithvi Raj Chauhan— Foolish belief of Hindu Guides

Sant Ji Maharaj used to narrate the story of Prithvi Raj Chauhan, in order to show as to how foolish religious beliefs were responsible for making India a slave country under the Muslim rulers for hundreds of years. He said, "Prithvi Raj Chauhan was so strong that Shahabuddin could never win him. But the Hindu leaders of that time misled Prithvi Raj Chauhan by asserting baseless beliefs. In the first war Shahabuddin was badly defeated; but when he attacked India for the second time, he joined hands with the enemies of India (Jai Chand and his men). They advised Shahabuddin to bring some cows in front of his armies and then Prithvi Raj Chauhan would not attack, fearing the so-called curse, as believed by Brahmans. They told Prithvi Raj Chauhan not to kill the cows and so Shahabuddin won the war and over-ran India. The Brahmans forgot that during the war the political advice must prevail over foolish religious beliefs. The so-called protectors of Hindu Religion saved a few thousand cows but this defeat resulted in massacre of crores of cows and of poor Hindu children, women and men. Then all kinds of unheard atrocities on helpless Indians were committed by Muslim Rulers. Sant Ji also observed, "The main cause of foreign rule in India and the commission of all kinds of atrocities on Hindus were due to most clever, selfish, short-sighted and bigoted Hindu guides."

Teaching of the lesson of the Divine Knowledge etc. While in Dal Lake—World is mere mirage

One day, when the boat of Sant Ji reached the middle of Dal Lake in Kashmir, its water was quite calm. No wind was blowing. The shadows of the surrounding mountains were very clear. It looked that these mountains 'existed' in the Dal Lake also. Sant Ji then taught a very important lesson and observed, "Just as the mountains seen in the Lake, in fact, do not exist, in the same way, in the boundless Oceans of Akash (the apparent canopy over the universe). This world is a mere mirage." These magical Divine Words of Sant Ji Maharaj penetrated the minds of all.

Obey the Divine Will—True Meditation by closing the eyes is most difficult

One day, Sant Ji Maharaj got a Supernatural Wave to leave Kashmir at once. Immediately, Bhai Thakar Singh, who had come from Amritsar to Sri Nagar, met Sant Ji and submitted, "Maharaj, all parties have gathered at Amritsar, for holding a conference. Kindly grace it by your presence." Sant Ji Maharaj accepted this request.

He went to Amritsar. After the morning Diwan at Gurdwara Babe-Di-Ber Sahib, the Manager of the

Gurdwara requested all to repeat Gurmantar (Waheguru) in their minds and make prayers that the Sikhs, who were in jails, might be released. The Sangat closed their eyes for nearly two minutes and then they began looking at each other. On this, Sant Ji Maharaj observed, "It is no good that on one side you talk ill of True Saints, who practise meditation, and you loudly proclaim that this is not the true way i.e., the closing one's eyes, then you say that he, who does not go to jail is not a Sikh, while now you are urging the Sangat to make prayers and get the Sikhs in jails released. Dear Sikhs, it is better to obey the Divine Will. In whatever way Satguru wants us to live is good for us." Then he quoted some verses.

Then he observed, "To fight mutually and pulling wires in different directions is not good. The Satguru is pained to see all this. Now tell which side the Satguru should take and whom he should help ?" On hearing this, the Manager begged pardon.

The man-made poems are false, the Gurbani alone is True and Divine

One day, at Jammu, in evening Diwan, the Sangat was absorbed in singing Divine Hymns, as usual. At that time, a Sadhu playing on his small instrument with one string, and singing some song (Bhajan) came there. Sant Ji did not take notice of him. On this he became angry and said, "Why have you not stopped singing, on my coming here ?" Sant Ji observed, "Bhai Sahib, I sing the Divine Hymns of Satguru Nanak Dev Ji, which came from the Supreme Being. Your Bhajans are man-made poems and are not permanent. I cannot show disrespect to Gurbani." This had magical effect on the Sadhu, who then sat in Diwan and was over-joyed to hear the Kirtan.

True Sikhs can be counted on fingers—Final Prayer should not be long

One day, when Sant Ji enquired as to what was the number of the Sikhs according to the latest census, which was being held. The answer was, "Sikhs are lacs according to the census." On this, Sant Ji observed, "I see only a few Khalsas amongst the Sikhs." Then he quoted the verses of the Tenth Satguru.

One day, at Gujranwala, the Diwan was held in the Kothi of Malik Hardit Singh, the then Deputy Commissioner of Gujranwala. After the Bhog, Sant Ji directed Malik Sahib to perform final prayer (Ardas). He submitted, "Maharaj, I can utter a short and not a long Ardas." Sant Ji Maharaj, on this, observed, "It is good. Ardas should not be very lengthy." Malik Sahib then uttered the Ardas. First he read the names of the Ten Satgurus and then rememberd Sri Guru Granth Sahib, the Lord of the four Takhats. Then he uttered the names of the Five Beloveds and of the respected four sons of the Tenth Satguru and then closed the Ardas with proper words. Sant Ji Maharaj was much pleased at this and observed, "Ardas should not be long. When Ardas is being performed, all the Ten Satgurus come there and stand on their toes till the Ardas is finished. If Ardas is long, this causes unnecessary discomfort to them."

Internal message of Bhai Atma Singh received by Sant Ji Maharaj

When Sant Ji was at Amritsar, one Sindhi old lady brought a blind devotee Bhai Atma Singh, by holding his arm. He placed his forehead on the feet of Sant Ji. A strange wave of affection and devotion came in his mind and he did not leave the feet of Sant Ji. Tears continued to flow. Sant Ji said many words of consolement and told him to raise his head. But the extreme true love of Bhai Atma Singh for Sant Ji was being exhibited and he could not control himself. The entire Sangat sitting there were greatly influenced by the sincere conduct of Bhai Atma Singh and exclaimed, "In this dark age, when people have become irreligious due to the so-called Western civilisation, it is very difficult to find a lover of Truth like him." After some time, Bhai Atma Singh controlled himself and with folded hands submitted, "This humble dog (slave) of yours had a strong yearning to have your Sight, since long. I used to pray that before I leave this world I may see you. Due to this internal attraction I came to Amritsar. Day and night I was thinking as to when that lucky time would come when I will place my forehead on your Lotus Feet. Blessed are you, who have come to know my internal message, sent to you by me and have so kindly afforded me time to see you. Now my desire has been fulfilled and I will spend my remaining life to merge my mind and attention in the Shabad (the Name) as directed by you." Sant Ji Maharaj fully consoled him and narrated the story of his past continuous services, rendered by him in his previous life. He observed, "Bhai Atma Singh is my old Sewak (devoted follower). With the Grace of the Satguru his true love will flourish unabated till the end of his life and will bear fruits."

After Bhai Atma Singh left, Sant Ji left Amritsar immediately. Regarding the rival parties amongst Sikhs, he observed, "The fire of mutual fights and envy amongst different groups is raising. I will not take part in their bickerings. I came for the sake of Bhai Atma Singh and now I am going back."

A True Saint is supposed by the devotees to be a 'bullock' to fulfil their desires—This is not correct— The True Saint tells the correct way and then it is for the devotee to gain benefits by following it

One day, after the morning Diwan, Sant Ji observed, "People want that the Sant should serve them as a bullock. When one goes to a city, situated at a sea-shore then one will see huge drums of steel standing on some parts of the sea, through which a ship has to pass. The concerned persons first search and examine carefully the parts of the sea, where rocks and sand dumps, and marshes etc. lie, hidden under the waters, and then they fix these drums at those places, so that a ship may not go that way and should take the safe line. A ship, which goes the right way is saved. Similarly those, who have already crossed this world sea (who have won the war against mammon; i.e. the True Saints) give true guidance to the worldly seekers after Truth, who are told that there are rocks of ego, then there are 'marshes' of false love, then there are whirlpools of anger, sex and greed. If the devotee travels after saving himself from these dangers, he crosses the world ocean. True Saints show true ways. It is for the devotee to travel on these."

One should fix his mind internally on The Kirtan, when Divine Hymns are being sung—Real Object of Kirtan explained

One day, a big Diwan was being held at Patiala at a place, from where the Railway line was not far off. During the performance of the Kirtan, the Sangat was hearing it with attached minds. All of a sudden, a goods train passed near that place. Most of the audience began seeing the train. Sant Ji stopped the Kirtan and observed,

"The real purpose of the Kirtan is that the mind may become detached from the worldly objects and should remain fixed, with the internal self. An ordinary thing, which you daily see, has caused your minds to go astray. This is not good at all. Take courage and be strong enough, so that your attention and mind may remain continuously fixed on the Shabad. Once, Satguru Kalgidhar was holding his Diwan at Anandpur Sahib. Bullets were being fired by the enemy from various directions. One bullet passed near a Singh, who lifted his knee, due to fear. The Satguru said, "It is the religious duty of a Sikh that he must not detract his mind from the Kirtan, although a bullet may pierce his body. If death comes during Kirtan, it is a very fortunate event. He, who allows, during Kirtan, any part of his body to move is an accursed person." The entire Sangat heard all these Sermons with full attention and after this never allowed the mind to go astray, from the Kirtan, although trains used to run near that place.

The 'Internal Diamond' is True and most Pure, but the External Diamond is False

Bhai Hira Singh was extremely ill. Due to his internal prayers, Sant Ji went to Delhi from Patiala. Sant Ji met him and said, "Bhai Hira Singh Ji, you were with me at Guru Sagar Sahib, Mastuana. You performed Sewa for nearly three years. I used to give you Sermons there as to how to obtain Nectarean Supernatural Joy and told you that you are not your body but your internal self i.e., the human soul is the 'Real Hira Singh'. Why did you not realise this, by practical meditation and worship etc. ?" Bhai Hira Singh submitted, "Maharaj, I used to preach this thing to the Sangat, but my mind never reached that height. Even when in the Diwan, someone scratched his head, I used to think that he was going to take out a rupee for giving it to me. Not only this, the Sadh Sangat used to get my services for collecting money there. For these reasons your teaching never bore practical results." Now Sant Ji Maharaj became extremely kind to him. A Supernatural Wave came in his mind. His face got a Special Brilliant 'Glow'. He then observed, "Bhai Hira Singh, even now nothing has been lost. Be brave and strong and fully believe, with determinantion that the Internal Hira Singh is True and the outer Hira Singh is false." When Sant Ji was saying this, the wife of Bhai Hira Singh in an affectionate tone submitted, "Maharaj, have mercy on him." Sant Ji Maharaj then, in his full Spiritual State said, "Bibi, I am doing so." Bhai Hira Singh fully understood this secret indication of Sant Ji Maharaj and he asked his emotional wife to keep quiet and to go out. Then Sant Ji, for the second time, with full force announced, "Bhai Hira Singh, the Internal Hira Singh is True and the outer Hira Singh is false." Feeling that his words had not full effect on Bhai Hira Singh, Sant Ji for the third time with greater force asserted the same Sermon and declared, "Hira Singh Ji, the Internal Diamod is True and outer one is false." After this, Sant Ji kept quiet and sat in meditation. After about two minutes Bhai Hira Singh with folded hands submitted, "O True King, my mind does not rise to that height."

Now, Sant Ji showered his Grace in a different way. He narrated the following story of Bhai Bhagtu :

"Bhai Bhagtu was a True Saint. When his end came very near, he got severe attack of dysentry. His followers, with folded hands, said to him, "You promised to get Liberation for us, but now you yourself have been caught in the net." On this, Bhai Bhagtu smiled and said, "O my friends, I used to give Sermons on the Sikh Religion in the backward regions. The residents of those places earned their livelihood by committing thefts. They used to steal she-camels of others and they used to give their milk to me for drinking. The accounts of these evil acts are to be rendered by me. I have prayed that these accounts may be settled in my this life and I may not take birth again to settle them, so I am undergoing this punishment."

After narrating the story, Sant Ji said, "Bhai Hira Singh Ji, we take food served by Sikhs. This food is procured by some by spending amounts etc. earned by them through honest means and by others by spending amounts etc. earned through sinful means. We have to render and settle accounts of this in this very birth, so that there is Liberation from future deaths and births." Sant Ji showered his grace on Bhai Hira Singh.

It is most difficult to win the mind

While explaining the working of the human mind, Sant Ji observed, "Brothers, it is most difficult to conquer the mind. Sometimes it looks to be dead, but then again it becomes alive. Until this mind, like a seed is not burnt in the fire of detachment and yearning for meeting the Beloved God, its small green part may again sprout. There is no difference in the shape of baked seed and green seed, so far as appearances are concerned. But the burnt and baked seed cannot grow, while the other will sprout. The seeker must be very cautious. The worldly people are very clever. The self-willed ones try to bring to their level virtuous persons, just as a marks-man will hit at a flying bird and cause its fall. This mind flies to heights, but it falls down on the ground just as a flying kite, when it sees a piece of meat lying on the ground quickly flies down from the sky and catches it. The mind after a good deal of meditation and religious practices believes that its evil desires are dead; but even a small worldly temptation may cause it to turn it into its former state. You must not put your trust on the flimsy mind, because it, many times, becomes active just as a snake hidden under the grass who comes out and bites others."

Greed-Acts done under the influence of greed, cause the seeker to be put in fetters and chains (i.e. result in his transmigration)

One day, Sant Ji Maharaj made observations regarding the effects of greed. He said, "Those who follow their minds yet wrongly think that they have become free, live in a fools' paradise. As long as the mind does not become fully self-contented and does not discard its evil and sinful ways and does not rise above the evil tastes of sex and tongue, it continues to be a slave. It faces punishments and pains just as a spider gets caught in its own net."

Success of Khalsa—The day, the Guru Khalsa honestly and impartially chooses leader and follows them, success in all spheres will follow the Khalsa

One day, some Akalis came and submitted to Sant Ji, "Maharaj, the Panth has become disrupted. How can unity be achieved ?" Sant Ji replied, "All the warring groups should present themselves before the

Akal Takhat Sahib and should perform Kirtan daily. The Shabad will bring Unity." Then the Akalis submitted, "Kindly let us know the worldly ways." Sant Ji again observed, "The day when the Guru Khalsa selects five leaders and one chief and when all will obey them, all projects, schemes and works etc., will be successfully performed. However (while making selection) honesty and impartiality must be exercised. None should be patronised. Whatever is in the minds must come out. But when once selection has been made all must obey them till they are alive and they must strictly observe the laws and rules laid down by the Satgurus. They must be obeyed. If you do not do this, then those who go high are thrown down on the ground."

CHAPTER XV

STORY OF THE MERGER OF THE HOLY SOUL OF SANT JI MAHARAJ WITH THE SUPREME SOUL AND OF HIS REACHING THE PALACE OF THE SATGURU—HIS LAST SERMONS

Sant Ji Maharaj was at Delhi. He attended a big congregation of Sangat at Gurdwara Bangla Sahib. He took his seat behind Guru Granth Sahib on the dais. It was the rainy season of Bhadon (August). Due to hot and stuffy atmosphere, the stage was set up outside, in the open. When after the Long Prayer (closing Ardas) Sant

Ji Maharaj sat on the dais, a small most poisonous snake bit him on his foot. A snake-charmer came and he followed his own way to cure the effects of the poison. This was the proper remedy. But some devotees insisted that the doctor must be called for proper treatment. They arrived at the scene and wanted to make Sant Ji senseless by administering chloroform, in order to perform a major operation. Sant Ji observed, "There is no need for chloroform. You may do anything with my body. I am not my body. You may cut any part you like. I will not feel pain. Do not worry at all."

Then two doctors started the operation. They applied their knives etc., for nearly one and a half hours. But Sant Ji remained lying in perfect comfort. His face had the same Divine Glow. He did not feel any pain whatsoever. The operation, however, did not succeed. Sant Ji's order that he should be taken to Balewal was complied with. At Balewal, a snake-charmer again started his treatment. It had good effects, but again the rich devotees brought doctors for treatment. They came and could not succeed in curing the wounds.

One day, Sant Ji observed, "As ordered by the Satguru Kalgidhar Ji Maharaj, I travelled throughout the Punjab and India. Lacs of people took Khande-Da-Amrit. Very big Diwans were held. Some appreciated my face and others my beard. Some praised my continuous meditation and some loved my sweet and loud voice. However, none asked me (except a few devotees) to let them know the True and Real Thing. Only such devotees happened to be the Seekers and Purchasers of the Taste of the Divine Nectar of the Name. All others thought that the life of a True Saint is a joke. I am not the body, that you see. This is my confirmed belief and it is a fact. All of you also train your minds to reach this Divine Height. Soul is one and the same and so there is no difference between you and me. Due to our attachment with the body, we feel pains etc."

After some days officers of the Jind Darbar took Sant Ji to Sangrur. There the Doctors and the Chief Minister tried their best to persuade Sant Ji to agree to get operated. He said, "There is no need of any operation. I am healthy. This Drama is played under the Will of Akal Purkh." They insisted on getting one more operation performed. The operation was performed, but without success. Sant Ji was quite calm and in Perfect Peace. After this, he said to the attendants, "I am going to dip deep Within Myself and will reach the Fourth State, above the physical self. None of you should at all try to give me any food or liquid etc., and you must not touch me. I will remain absorbed in the Divine Spiritual State. Whatever is the Order and Will of the Creator, will come into the effect at the proper time."

Now this Great Divine and Perfect Saint, who had reformed lacs of persons, was sitting in the lap of the Satguru Kalgidhar Sahib in the most Spiritual Fourth State. At about 1 a.m., the night of 19th Magh, Sammat 1963 (1st February, 1927) he went to the Home of Waheguru and Satgurus, leaving lacs of devotees weeping in extreme grief.

The Holy body of Sant Ji Maharaj coverved with very costly shawls etc., placed in a beautiful flower-bedecked bier, after performing full ceremonies according to Gurmat, was brought in a huge procession to Mastuana Sahib (Gur Sagar). Chandanwood pyre was already made, on which his holy body was placed. Thousands of Sangat collected there. Fire was given to the pyre after recitation of Kirtan Sohila. Continuous Kirtan had already been started. Gurmat ceremonies were performed. At this place, a big Gurdwara with a big hall was constructed. One hundred and one Akhand Paths of Sri Guru Granth Sahib were performed at Gur Sagar Sahib. The countless devotees also got many Akhand Paths performed at their respective places.

he two ... Kalın ... continuous ...
... han had slowly been ... had a further ... ...
... were ... which ... ... the ... with ...
... was ... with ... ... the ... ...
... ... and it also
... ... The ... ...
... ... by reason of the ... use of a place ...